THE LAND AND PEOPLE OF INDONESIA

The Land and People
of
INDONESIA

By Datus C. Smith, Jr.

PORTRAITS OF THE NATIONS SERIES

J. B. Lippincott Company
Philadelphia and New York

To my favorite Indonesians

Julia & Hassan,
Fatimah, Faridah, Amalia

CONTENTS

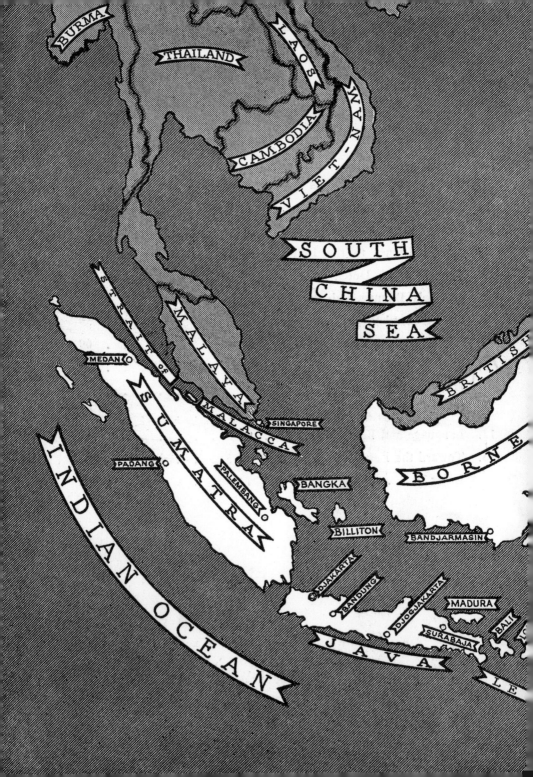

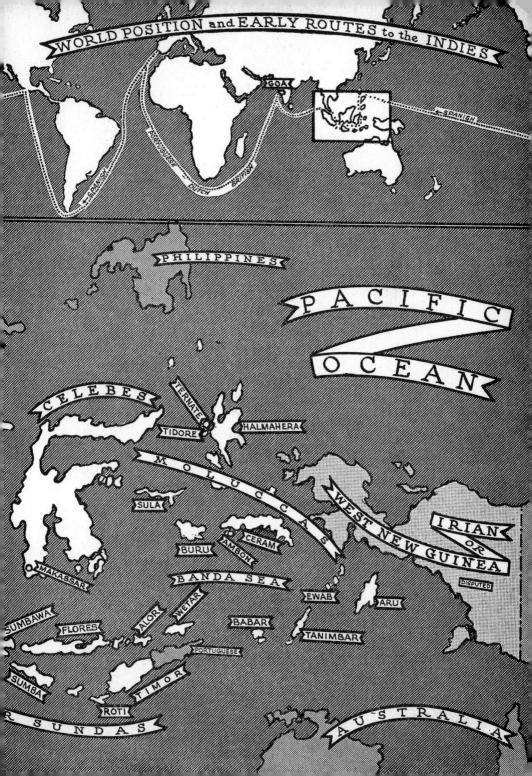

1

The Green Land and
Its People

Halfway around the globe from the United States, directly on the equator and between the continents of Asia and Australia, lies the green land of Indonesia.

It is so far away, and so new in world affairs, that Americans know little about the country, which has a place in geography like no other nation on earth.

Indonesia is not a solid land-mass, but a vast cluster or archipelago of more than three thousand islands. Some are small ones of only a few square miles, but mighty Borneo is the third largest island in the world, and Sumatra is about a thousand miles from tip to tip.

The shores of these islands are washed by the Pacific and Indian Oceans and the South China Sea. Indonesia's nearest neighbors are Singapore and Malaya to the north, the Philippines to the northeast, and Australia to the southeast.

The Republic of Indonesia declared its independence only in 1945, and so we often think the country is little because it is so young as a free nation. This introduction to the land and people should therefore start with two facts about the country's breathtaking size:

1. By population, Indonesia is the sixth largest country in the world. Only China, India, Soviet Union, United States, and Japan have more people than Indonesia's estimated eighty-nine million.

2. The distance from one end of Indonesia to the other is greater than from New York to San Francisco, while the north-and-south distance is about the same as from Minneapolis to New Orleans.

But it is not only the size that holds our interest. This is the fabled land of "the Indies." Here are the Spice Islands of history and romance. This is an area associated with such names as Marco Polo, Kublai Khan, Magellan, Sir Francis Drake, St. Francis Xavier, and the daring voyagers of the Age of Discovery. Here was the pomp and ceremony in the courts of the great Javanese kings. This was the onetime empire of the Dutch. Still today, even in this time of jet travel, Indonesia is one of the most picturesque and colorful places on earth.

The physical setting of Indonesian life is dramatic. Many of the great mountains are volcanoes, and this area is known as the most volcanic region of the world. In dense green jungles on the mountainsides, or on the plains or in the swamps below, are such wildlife as monkeys, tigers, rhinoceroses (almost extinct), thirty-foot pythons, wild boars, crocodiles, strange birds of handsome plumage, and an endless variety of small animals and insects of the most delicate beauty.

Some of the land is so fruitful that an entire family can live on the produce of a plot smaller than an American farmer would think worth planting. The whole year is a growing season in this tropical region, so a piece of land may produce three crops a year.

Exotic plant life is everywhere. Rice is the chief food for many of the people, and the rice paddy on plains or terraces is typical of the

Indonesian scene. Coconut trees grow by the million, and one constantly sees bamboo, papaya, and banana.

For much of the time in recent years, Indonesia has been the biggest producer of natural rubber in the world. Most of it is grown on huge rubber plantations owned by companies. Other plantations grow sugar cane, palm oil, tobacco, coffee, tea, and cinchona (the source of the medicine quinine). Pepper comes from Indonesia, and so do other spices that we shall later see played a big role in the country's history. Tapioca, rattan, teakwood, and kapok (for upholstery) are other products. Delicious fruit is available in every season, and in varieties whose very names are unknown to us.

Beneath the soil is still more wealth. Oil is the most important mineral product, and it is a major factor in Indonesia's income from abroad. But also there are tin, some coal, and bauxite (the source of aluminum), and lesser amounts of salt, manganese, nickel, gold, silver, and other metals. Iron resources, possibly of low grade, are believed to exist in considerable quantity, but they have not been developed.

Along the coastline, which is one of the longest in the world, and in the waters offshore, Indonesia draws on the riches of the ocean. Besides the growing fish industry on the seacoast, there is an inland fish culture by which fish are handled as a "crop" in ponds or in the waters of a rice paddy between crops of grain.

Green is the color of the landscape, with accents of brilliant flowers and flowering trees and, in some sections, the red-tile roofs of houses.

Plant life is of amazing variety. Wild orchids grow as parasites on trees in the jungle and on backyard racks in the cities. There are giant ferns as tall as trees. The banyan, a species of fig, seeds itself in a crotch of another tree, putting down roots to the ground; eventually the other tree is destroyed, leaving the fig high in the air, supported by aerial roots that come down from its branches, making eerie caverns of the space they enclose. Fantastic vines called lianas have been known to grow to the thickness of a man's thigh and to lengths of hundreds of feet.

The largest flower in the world, rafflesia, is a native of Indonesia and the bloom is sometimes three feet across. A pond in the beautiful botanical gardens at Bogor has many handsome lily pads more than five feet wide.

Plenty of rain and steady warmth keep things green in much of the country. Some sections have no dry season at all. Bogor, a small city near Djakarta, has an average of more than 300 thunderstorms each year. Some places have a rainfall of 160 inches per year (New York, which is considered well off, has 42 inches).

Too continuous a rainfall can be harmful, because thick jungle swamps of mangrove trees are no help to man. Also, even aside from the swamps, vegetation grows so fast that unless there is ceaseless effort, land cleared for farming returns quickly to its jungle state. But in quite a bit of Indonesia the amount of rain is exactly right. In such places, as on the island of Java, there is almost unbelievable fertility of a useful sort.

Because of the nearness of the sea, the actual thermometer reading is lower than we might expect in the tropics. In eighty years of record-keeping in Djakarta the highest temperature in history was 96 degrees, and the average is about 80. Even so, the steaming heat in low-lying areas seems to the foreign visitor to be almost impossible to bear when he first meets it. Morning and evening humidity are almost always in the 90's. At higher altitudes, however, the temperature and humidity are lower and the air more bracing.

Indonesia's place on the equator makes the temperature in any one place about the same all the year round. In many sections not more than three degrees separate the average of the warmest from the coolest month. Seasonal change is much less than that resulting from height above sea level. The thermometer may drop about one degree for each three hundred feet above the sea.

Also, because of the equatorial position there is a difference of less than an hour between the longest and shortest days of the year, as compared with nearly six hours difference in the latitude of New York.

The land is rich, especially in some of the islands, and yet the people are very poor because there are so many of them. It is hard to learn exactly what is the income per person in countries such as Indonesia where home-grown food may be more important for many families than income in the form of money. Even if we make big allowance for this, however, it is certain that Indonesians are among the poorest people on earth. Different studies put the value of the average Indonesian's income for a whole year at $15 to $40.

Some people think that, because of the growing population, the situation will become worse. Others are hopeful that, if political problems can be solved, and if some kind of balance can be found between growth of population and increase of food supply, life could become better. These people put their faith in reclaiming waste land, in improving the yield of crops, especially rice, and further advance in the growing of fish, in building up industries, aided by electricity from water power, in a movement to the islands that are less thickly settled, and in a slowing down of the rate of increase of population.

The center of Indonesian national life is on the remarkable island of Java, with which the small island of Madura is usually associated. In an area about the size of Alabama (about nine per cent of Indonesia's land area) something like fifty-eight million people live on Java-Madura. It is one of the most highly cultivated spots on earth. Ingenious systems of irrigation have helped nature's own generosity so much that the land supports more than 1,100 people to the square mile—which compares with about 50 to the square mile for the United States, 150 for Indonesia as a whole, and not more than 350 for India, which is tragically overpopulated.

As in all countries, in Indonesia the population is more interesting than anything else. These sturdy and attractive brown-skinned people are intelligent, industrious (when they see the reason for work), basically gentle and tolerant, and very, very patient. In fact, as we shall see later, if it were not for this remarkable quality of patience the country might not have survived its seemingly endless political troubles.

The majority of the people are of a stock called Indonesian or Malay, but with some mixture of blood of Indian origin, as well as bits of Chinese, Arab, and European.

More than nine-tenths of the people are Muslim in religion, that is, followers of Mohammed, the Arab prophet of Islam. His teachings in the Holy Koran came to these remote islands through trading vessels in past centuries. But the influence of Hindu, Buddhist, and even earlier beliefs is still strong. And Western influence through the Portuguese, British, Dutch, and more recently other Europeans and Americans, can be seen in religion, education, business, and science. At least in the cities it is also evident in such details of daily life as movies, DDT, lipstick, and Coca-Cola.

The way of life of the Indonesians is highly varied. In the capital city of Djakarta, which has a population of more than three million, are intellectuals who read the *New York Times,* play classical hi-fi, and talk casually about when they were last in Chicago, Paris, or London. In Borneo, in contrast, are tribes just a few steps from the Stone Age, living by the most primitive agriculture and by hunting and fishing.

It is with good reason that the country has as its national motto the words *Bhinneka Tunggal Ika,* meaning "Unity in Diversity," which is just about like our own *E Pluribus Unum,* "One Out of Many."

Love of independence is of course the strongest force holding the parts of the country together. Another is the Muslim religion, combined with tolerance of other beliefs. But something needing special mention is the national language.

There are more than two hundred languages spoken in family and village life. But a single national language came to general use as part of the independence movement.

We shall discuss this in Chapter 12, but the reader might like to know now how to pronounce the few Indonesian words in this book.

Most letters are pronounced about as you might guess, but there are
four rules worth learning:

J   is pronounced like Y   in "Yes"
Dj is pronounced like J   in "Jay"
Sj is pronounced like Sh in "Shop"
Tj is pronounced like Ch in "Chip"

The Dutch, and sometimes Americans, spell the capital city "Jakarta,"
but that would mean pronunciation as "Yakarta," so the Indonesians
give it as Djakarta. We shall follow their spelling in this book. (Exceptions: we shall use Sumatra and Java, which are familiar to us,
instead of the Indonesian "Sumatera" and "Djawa.")

After independence, English replaced Dutch as Indonesia's official
foreign language, and there is rapidly growing knowledge of our
language among the educated classes.

Indonesians have an absolute passion for education. Denial of the
chance for most of them to learn during the rule of other countries
has made them especially eager for education, now that they are
running their own affairs.

Before independence only about seven per cent of the Indonesians
could read and write, and a mere handful had a higher education. Few
members of the older generation were well enough trained to qualify
for senior leadership of this great country, and that has made it hard
to organize the life and work of the Republic. Old and young are
determined that the new generation will be literate, educated, and,
as required, technically trained.

Though few could read and write, there have been other forms of
cultural life throughout the centuries. Although these were actually
more intricate than mere reading and writing, they required no formal
training in school classrooms. These were the wonderful arts of music,
dance, theater, sculpture, painting, architecture, batik-making which
continued right through the whole period of foreign rule.

The Republic has survived periods of great trouble, to the surprise
of much of the world. Getting independence was in itself a glowing
achievement. But thus far the country has not worked out a stable

and effective political system. Governing yourself is always a harder job than breaking loose from foreign control.

In our own early history, the end of the War of Independence was the beginning of a difficult period. Indonesia, likewise, has been troubled by indifference, bad management, inefficiency, dishonesty, and the selfish interests of special groups and regions. And Indonesia has had special problems we never knew, because the pressure of world politics is far greater in this age.

But Indonesia has gone right on through crisis after crisis. There is reason for hoping that, no matter what may happen in the immediate future, these wonderful people will come out serenely on the other side of their difficulties. They have a shining goal in the ideals of their Republic. These are the famous Five Principles whose symbols are on the national coat-of-arms: nationalism, sovereignty of the people, humanitarianism or internationalism, social justice, and belief in God.

To learn the history of this green land, and the achievements and problems and hopes of its people, we should turn back to the beginning of its history. But first a quick survey of the geography will help us understand the story as it unfolds.

2

Islands in the Sea

The thousands of islands making up the Indonesian archipelago are divided in different ways by geographers. For us it is perhaps easiest to think of them in four groups:

1. *The Western Islands* of Sumatra, Borneo, and Java.
2. *The Lesser Sunda Islands,* a chain running eastward from the end of Java toward Australia.
3. *The Eastern Islands,* including Celebes and the many islands of the Moluccas group, which stretches up toward the Philippines.
4. *Western New Guinea,* which the Indonesians dispute with the Dutch, who now hold it.

Among those main groups we can see differences in plants, animals, soil, people, and general culture. And beneath the ground and under the seas is the record of difference in geological history.

The islands in the west, Sumatra, Java, and Borneo, are set in shallow seas, often only two hundred feet deep, and much of the land along their shores is swamp and marsh. This suggests what the geolo-

17

gists say is a fact: that these major western islands were part of the Asian mainland not too many thousand years ago. In fact, this part of Indonesia might be considered still part of the mainland, even though portions of it are buried under a few hundred feet of water.

The islands to the east of this continental shelf, however, are the tops of incredibly steep mountains going right up from the floor of very deep seas. In some cases there is a difference in altitude of thirty thousand feet between an ocean deep and an island mountain-top not a hundred miles away. This region is geologically "young," and mountain-building is still going on. Earthquakes are frequent, and there are two or three mild tremors every day, as well as occasional severe ones.

Volcanoes are in a great crescent-shaped line going the length of Sumatra and Java and then sweeping northward into the Philippines. There are more than a hundred active volcanoes in the country, about half of them in Java, and countless dead cones from former times. At the bottom of Sumatra is a tiny island that is all that is left of one of the world's most famous volcanoes. This is Krakatoa, which blew up in 1883, destroying much of the island and causing tidal waves and dust clouds that circled the globe. A new eruption produced a little island of volcanic ash in 1928, and it is called Anak Krakatoa (child of Krakatoa).

The volcanoes are so dramatic that they interest us for their own sake, but they also give the key to all life in Indonesia. There are two kinds of lava that come from volcanoes. The sort called "acid" makes waste land that is very poor for growing things. But the sort called "basic" gives a rich soil on which crops thrive.

The wonderful productivity of Java, and of parts of other islands, results from the deep layers of volcanic soil, plus the steady rainfall and warmth. The areas that are the richest in agriculture tend to become the richest culturally and the strongest politically. So we might say that the enormous power of volcanoes when they are active is not lost, but continues to affect the life of the people for centuries after they themselves are cold and quiet.

The main features of the Indonesian landscape, aside from the changes made in it by man, are the mountains, the tropical "rain forests" that are the same the year round, a few "monsoon forests" with some seasonal change, the "swamp forests" along the flat shorelines and sometimes continuing far inland, and the areas of brushy grassland or "savannah." This last is a flat land with few trees and little vegetation except shrubs and giant grasses. Such areas are of little natural use to man, and the same is true of the jungle swamps.

Because Java is so thickly populated, there has been an effort to get Javanese to emigrate to other islands, especially Sumatra and Borneo, where there is much empty space. It is thought that some of the present waste land could be adapted to support people, just as parts of the Great American Desert in our Southwest were converted to man's use. The movement out from Java has not yet been very great, however, and has by no means kept up with the population growth on Java itself. We mentioned earlier that more than 1,100 people to the square mile live on Java; in Sumatra the density is only about 78 and in Borneo 18.

Let us take a quick tour around the islands where the eighty-nine million Indonesians live, starting with the upper lefthand corner of the map.

Sumatra, about a thousand miles long, has mountains along its west side, close to the shore. The eastern side slopes down to flat savannah and marshes, though with many big areas that man has learned to put to his use. For instance, in the section called Deli near the city of Medan, scientists learned how to grow on former waste land the special kind of Sumatran tobacco that has high value in world trade. In the southern part of the island there have been big developments in growing irrigated rice, much as in Java; and great plantations of rubber, sugar, and other commercial crops are also found on Sumatra.

The island is one of the major sources of oil in Indonesia, and smaller islands off its coast, especially Bangka and Billiton, produce large amounts of tin.

There are about fifteen million Sumatran people and they are of very different sorts. At the northern end of the island are the people of Atjeh whose rugged independence we shall mention later. Somewhat below them are the Batak, who have a different culture and language, and many of whom are Christians. About halfway down the island on the west side are the remarkable Minangkabau people whom we will meet again in this book. At the southern end is a mixture of tribes and languages. The cities of the island of more than two hundred thousand population are Medan, Palembang, and Padang.

Borneo (which the Indonesians call Kalimantan) does not have many great mountains, but much of it is hilly and forested. Borneo as a whole is the third largest of all islands (it follows Greenland and New Guinea), but not all of it belongs to Indonesia. Along the northern edge are three British territories, Sarawak, Brunei (which means Borneo), and North Borneo. Oil and rubber are produced in both the British and Indonesian parts of the island. In the west there is an area of farmland worked by descendants of Chinese who came in originally as gold miners.

There are only about four million people in Borneo's huge area. Through much of the northern and central parts the people are Dayaks, with a language of their own and living a quite primitive life of hunting, fishing, and "shifting agriculture." That is, they will clear and plant ground, raise crops there for a few years, and then move on after the natural chemicals are exhausted. Of the few cities on the whole island, Bandjarmasin is the largest, about one hundred seventy-five thousand.

Java is by all odds not only the richest and most populous (fifty-eight million including Madura) of all the islands, but one of the lushest and most densely populated places on earth. A great volcanic chain of mountains runs the length of the island. In certain sections some of the area is lost to waste land, but elsewhere there is a marvelous development of rice terraces, plantations of sugar, tea, coffee, rubber, and other crops.

The people called Javanese and using the Javanese language are at the extreme western tip and in much of the eastern two-thirds. Between those two sections, in western Java, is an area, especially around the city of Bandung, of the Sundanese people. At the extreme eastern end, and on the island of Madura which fits into a notch of northeast Java, are the Madurese people with their own culture and language.

Indonesia's four major cities are on Java. Djakarta (formerly called Batavia by the Dutch) is the national capital. It has a population of over three million, making it one of the biggest cities in the world. Like New York, Djakarta has attracted people from so many other parts of the country and from abroad that it has a true cosmopolitan spirit and a culture of its own.

Many Indonesians, as well as foreigners, criticize Djakarta and say they certainly would hate to live there, just as many Americans criticize New York, believing that it represents some of the worst aspects of the country. There is surely less natural courtesy and friendliness, less gracious adjustment to the problems of living, in those huge cities than in some of the country areas or smaller towns in both countries. The next largest city is Surabaja, with more than a million people, at the eastern end of Java. The pleasant city of Bandung, whose special reason for world fame we mention in the final chapter, has nearly a million people. Semarang, about half that size, is the fourth largest.

Although Djogjakarta (which foreigners sometimes mistake for a fancy spelling of Djakarta) is somewhat smaller; it is important in our story, as it was the capital of the Republic during the revolution.

Going eastward from Java, we come to the Lesser Sunda chain of islands which the Indonesians call Nusa Tenggara. First is the beautiful island of Bali, which many people think is as close to paradise as they are likely to come before going to heaven. This is the one part of Indonesia still Hindu in religion. The distinctive culture and delightful scenery have made it one of the great tourist attractions in the Far East. As we shall see in other chapters, Balinese architecture, music, dance, costuming, carving, and textiles are famous all over the world.

Working eastward along the chain, we go from Bali to Lombok, Sumbawa, Sumba, Flores, Timor, and many smaller islands. The eastern half of Timor is Portuguese, the only surviving trace in the Indies of Portugal's imperialist effort of the fifteenth and sixteenth centuries. There are no large cities in the Lesser Sundas, and the total population is less than six million.

In the islands in the northeast quarter of the country, the biggest unit is Celebes, which the Indonesians call Sulawesi. It is the most curiously shaped large island in the world. Some people say it looks like an orchid. Its far-flung arms go out in such odd directions that for many years early European traders thought it was a group of islands rather than one piece. The country is very mountainous, and both plants and animals include varieties found nowhere else in the world. The principal city is Makassar, on the southwest arm, once a center of spice smuggling. Total population of Celebes is about six and a half million.

In the Moluccas, the Spice Islands of bygone times, the biggest is Halmahera, with a shape almost as odd as Celebes, and another large island is Ceram. The island of Ambon, near Ceram, is not large but was important in history, even in the final Dutch period, when it was the site of a principal naval base captured by the Japanese. Total population of the Moluccas is less than a million.

Christian missions were set up in the Moluccas very early, and the missionaries had some effect on cultural life. In the islands that are heavily Christian there has been change in the form of folk art, and some of the traditional forms of music and the dance have been lost. Even long periods of Christian influence, however, have failed to wipe out many familiar customs and beliefs.

The final section of the archipelago, called Irian by the Indonesians, is the western half of the island of New Guinea. The eastern half is held by Australia. In the agreement in 1949 about the other islands, Holland and Indonesia were not able to settle whether Western New Guinea also would become part of Indonesia, so it was left for later agreement. Holland continued to hold the area, but Indonesia pressed its claim in the United Nations and elsewhere. Holland refused to negotiate, but told the UN in 1960 that it would abide by the results of an eventual vote of the New Guinea people.

The Indonesians' familiar name for their great country is "Tanah Air Kita," which means "Our land and water." We have had a very quick bird's-eye view of that huge area of islands and seas, and shall now turn to its history.

3

From the Beginning

The story of man in Indonesia is one of the oldest in the world, and its beginning may be traced from thousands of years before history was written. Almost from the first there are signs of at least some of the characteristics that we see in Indonesia today.

Southeast Asia, the region in which Indonesia is the largest and most important country, has not usually played a big role in world affairs in its own right. But it has served through many centuries as a meeting place of races, cultures, religions, languages, and commerce. And World War II was only one of many times when military forces from outside the area fought with each other in Southeast Asia.

Commerce is the key to much of the story. The modern American businessman going to Indonesia to sell penicillin or to buy rubber or tin, and the German businessman selling Volkswagens or buying tea, are in a tradition that has lasted for thousands of years. And contact through foreign trade explains much of the richness and variety in Indonesian culture.

How did it all start? No one can say exactly how man began on

24

earth, or the exact steps of evolution that led to the earliest form of *Homo sapiens*, or where that happened first. It is no longer as certain as formerly that Asia was the birthplace of man, but it seems likely that tropical Southeast Asia was at least one of the places where the great evolutionary process occurred.

One of the figures in the drama even bears an Indonesian name. The so-called "Java Man," whose fossil remains were found in 1891, is perhaps the most famous of the pre-human forms known as *Pithecanthropus erectus*.

As our scientific knowledge has increased, and as the remains of other types have been found, in Java and elsewhere, much has been learned about these early creatures, and about the true human beings who followed them. Indonesia is a rich source for the earliest chapter of the human story.

Present-day Indonesians are not descendants of those earliest human inhabitants of their country, but rather of a people who came from the outside many thousands of years later. A series of great migrations into Southeast Asia has been traced by study of fossils, stone implements, and other remains of ancient culture.

Of those waves, the one that left the largest number of living descendants today, and indeed supplied the basic stock of the present Indonesian people, was a race appropriately called Indonesians.

The oldest of these Indonesians are believed to have come from southwest China, and to have moved about four thousand years ago into the land that is now the Indonesian archipelago. Scholars see that there were two types of those ancient Indonesians. The people in the second group are often called Coastal Malay, as they settled along the shore, while the earlier arrivals tended to keep to the highland interior.

For both types the terms "Indonesian" and "Malay" are often used interchangeably, and these people are of the racial type seen most often nowadays in Southeast Asia.

There was some connection of the ancient Indonesians with Mongol peoples in the homeland, and there is evidence of Chinese trade in the area of present-day Indonesia back to at least 100 B.C.

But India was more important than China in Indonesian history. The influence was stronger, and its effect was lasting. At the time of the first Chinese trade, or even earlier according to some experts, there was Indian trade and perhaps there were settlements of colonists from India. For some time Indian traders went to the islands in search of gold, silver, and tin, and eventually some of them decided to settle permanently.

For lack of formal history books to give the facts about this early contact, scholars turn to other sources. Evidence is given not only by the writing in Indian script on stone monuments in Sumatra and Java, but also by what appear to be references to the islands preserved in very old Indian literature.

By the seventh and eighth centuries A.D., kingdoms had grown up in Sumatra and Java with close connections with India. This remarkable Hindu-Indonesian civilization developed steadily, and then continued strong for nearly seven centuries, until the time of the general conversion to Muslim beliefs. In fact, the Hindu-Indonesian influence did not disappear with the coming of Islam, and it is still evident. It can be seen in many phases of Indonesian life right down to the present day. The name normally used for this culture is Hindu-Javanese, because Java was its center, but the Hindu influence spread to all the islands.

Traders and settlers from India brought not only Hinduism but also Buddhism. And Chinese traders, though less numerous, also brought Buddhist influence. It was in central Java during the eighth and ninth centuries A.D., under the kings called the Shailendras, that there was an absolute flower-burst of artistic activity. Architecture was one of the arts in which the Javanese excelled, and it is for some of the great buildings that Buddhism in Java is best remembered today.

The greatest of all the monuments in Indonesia, the mighty temple of Borobodur in Java, probably dates from this period, and gives the modern beholder a vivid feeling of the force that this religion exerted in Javanese life.

But we should not think of central Java in the Borobodur period as having become entirely Buddhist. During all of Indonesian history the lines dividing cultures and religions have been hazy. Old beliefs and old ways have continued in the Indies, no matter what religion was officially accepted. Each new religion took on some color of the old. And the former faith, where it continued, became modified to include parts of the new ritual or belief.

Political history of the islands is just as mixed. A kingdom would come to power in a local area, gain control of some neighboring territory, and then disappear or merge in a greater monarchy. A majority of the "kings" were no more than tribal chieftains, and their "nations" merely tribes able to exercise power over a nearby region for a little while. Some of the kingdoms, however, and especially those in Java and along the Strait of Malacca, lasted for longer periods, had influence in mainland Asia as well as in the islands, and showed all the pomp and elaborate ceremony of royal courts in a fairy tale.

One of the early kings deserving our notice even in this quick survey was King Airlangga of East Java, an eleventh-century monarch whose name is well known in Indonesia today, though he reigned shortly before the Norman Conquest of Britain. Legends about him are familiar to the common people, and Westerners call him an "Indonesian King Arthur." His name has been given to one of the leading universities of present-day Indonesia.

Another of the great names, in this case from the fourteenth century, is likewise used by a modern university. This is Gadjah Mada, prime minister of the kingdom of Madjapahit. He was one of the first statesmen in Indonesia in something like the modern meaning of the term. He had a vision of one country for all the islands, and did in fact succeed in bringing a large part of Indonesia under the rule of his king.

This Madjapahit Empire, which was probably the biggest Indonesian nation until the birth of the Republic six and a half centuries later, showed in its origin a familiar pattern of interference in Indonesian affairs by foreign countries. Time after time through history, world events, even if far away, have had strong effect in the islands. Foreign pressure has changed the course of Indonesian life many times. An example of this can be found at that early time, even before the coming of the first Europeans.

The fabulous Kublai Khan of China is the chief actor in this drama. Kublai was ruling a large section of mainland Asia from his picturesque court in Peking when, late in the thirteenth century, he started a drive to the south. It was a movement that later centuries would have called "imperialist expansion." Smaller nations were conquered or scared into submission, and then were included in a system of satellites. One after another they fell under Kublai's control.

But a king in Java, Kertanagara, refused to give in, and even offered to help a threatened neighbor. This and other Javanese signs of independence were too much for Kublai. He ordered an attack on the island kingdom.

More than two years went into getting ready for this amphibious operation which was to be the greatest military venture in Indonesia up to that time. Hundreds of vessels and more than twenty thousand troops were said to be involved.

When the attack finally came in 1293 it had a most unexpected result. King Kertanagara had died before the Chinese reached Java, so the invaders were not able to discipline the king as they had planned. They were, however, persuaded to help one of the parties that were fighting for the throne left vacant by Kertanagara's death. But then they were tricked into a position in which their large army, spread through the countryside, was ambushed by Javanese forces. Before long the Chinese felt they had enough of Indonesia, and their armada withdrew. The only result was that they had helped launch the powerful Madjapahit Empire, which was eventually guided to greatness by Gadjah Mada. Indonesia was not always so fortunate in disposing of invaders.

It was just a year or so before Kublai's attack on Java that the first European visited another of the islands. This was Marco Polo, one of the most famous travelers of all time. He was returning with his father from the court of the Great Khan in China when he touched at northern Sumatra.

Marco's visit is interesting to us not only as the first European presence in Indonesia, but because he noted in passing something that we now see was of great importance to the future of the islands. Marco wrote that although Sumatrans in general were pagan worshipers of idols, "many of those who dwell in the seaport towns have been converted to the religion of Mohammed by the Saracen merchants who constantly frequent them."

Muslim traders from the Persian Gulf and the Red Sea as well as from India had been making voyages to the Indies, for centuries before Marco's observation. As time went on, more and more came, some of them as settlers; this was especially true along the Strait of Malacca, the greatest trading channel of Southeast Asia.

Ports in Sumatra and Java were centers for exchanging goods between the East and the West. They dealt in the produce of China as well as of the islands. But the spices of the Molucca Islands, in the eastern part of present-day Indonesia, were what produced an excitement like a gold rush.

Enormous profits could be made from a single voyage. The taste of Europeans and Near Easterners demanded larger and larger amounts of pepper, cloves, and nutmeg, as well as rare herbs, scented woods, and the oils extracted from them. Some of these products of the Moluccas were found also in India or elsewhere, but for many of them there was not at that time a single other source known to man.

The produce of these Spice Islands was carried from the Indonesian trading centers to India. Then it went by overland caravan to bazaars in the Near East, and then on to Europe; or sometimes direct to Arab and Persian ports without using the overland route through India.

It was natural that the first strongly Muslim area should be right where Marco Polo saw it, along the Strait of Malacca. As the map shows, it is a narrow waterway between the island of Sumatra and the Malay Peninsula, the nearest part of mainland Asia. Any seafarer heading for the Spice Islands, or intending to turn northward to China, would naturally go "down the slot" of the Malacca Strait, right past the island at the tip of the Malay Peninsula that is the site of present-day Singapore (though the city itself did not come into being until centuries later).

As local rulers and chiefs along the Strait adopted the teachings of Mohammed's holy book, the general population followed them. In accordance with Indonesian custom, however, there was no clean break with the past. Indeed, there were Muslim mosques in the architectural form of Hindu-Javanese temples, and Muslim tombs bearing Hindu symbols.

By the end of the fourteenth century, the powerful kingdom of Malacca, alongside the Strait, was firmly committed to the Muslim faith. During the fifteenth century there was a rapid spread to many of the islands. From that time onwards, the Indies have been overwhelmingly Muslim, in spite of the centuries of Christian contact and the influence of the Portuguese, Dutch, and British. The island of Bali has stayed Hindu in spite of everything, and there are Christian sections in the country also. But the islands in general have been Muslim since the fifteenth century.

After the Indies had accepted Islam, and while Indians, Arabs, and Persians were busily engaged in the spice trade, western Europe was on the brink of the Age of Discovery. A shorter route to "the Indies" (that is, to the Molucca source of the spices) was one of the chief reasons for the perilous voyages undertaken by the Spanish, Portuguese, and English. As we know, the purely accidental result was discovery of America. Although the theory of reaching the East by sailing west was entirely sound, the first direct contact with Indonesia by European vessels came about in another way—by the eastward voyages of Portuguese ships around Africa.

The fifteenth-century Portuguese prince known as Henry the Navigator not only studied navigation and geography, but also sponsored voyages of exploration. Portuguese ships pushed down the west coast of Africa ever farther and, after Henry's death, went eastward around the Cape of Good Hope, then to the island of Madagascar, and finally, in 1498 under Vasco da Gama, across the Indian Ocean to India.

But the conquistador who really established Portugal's power in the Indian Ocean and beyond was the great admiral and governor, Alfonso de Albuquerque, whose name is as famous in Eastern history as Cortez and Pizarro in the West. Albuquerque set up the naval base at Goa, on the west coast of India, and from there undertook the conquest of Malacca. He it was who directed Portugal's boisterous entry into the Indonesian story.

Separate pieces of world history were beginning to come together. Albuquerque's attack on the kingdom of Malacca was not only a commercial venture but a kind of continuation of the Crusades. The Christians in the West had been battling Moors and Turks, so it seemed natural and proper for the Portuguese to continue the struggle against these other Muslims half a world away.

Whatever the religious tone, however, the real goals were the spices and other riches of the Indies. Possession of the "tollgate" of Malacca gave control of the trade from the Spice Islands and the sea-borne commerce of the Far East with India, the Middle East, and Europe.

At this time—about a hundred years before the Pilgrims reached Plymouth in the other half of the world—Portugal was the strongest power in the Indies.

4

Europe Comes to the Indies

Capture of the Muslim stronghold of Malacca alongside the Strait established the Portuguese with the powers of a tollgate-keeper, as we mentioned. It also put them conveniently near the pepper gardens of Sumatra. But the cloves and nutmegs of the Moluccas were still twenty-five hundred miles away.

(Because the names are confusingly similar, note the difference between Malacca and Moluccas. The former was the Muslim kingdom and its capital on the Malay Peninsula, not far from present-day Singapore. The latter are islands in the eastern part of Indonesia, the Spice Islands, original home of all the cloves and nutmegs in the world.)

The Portuguese made mistakes from the very beginning. They hated Islam and they had nothing but contempt for the Malays and Indonesians. Their first act after taking Malacca was utterly shocking to good Muslims: they built a fortress from Muslim gravestones. Then they staged a series of executions. Later their admiral undertook a campaign of general piracy in the Indian Ocean. From start to finish the adventurers left a record of brutality and betrayal. The British and

Dutch in their turn made costly errors also, but Portuguese action was often without reason. Political disaster came eventually, and finally loss of most of the commerce itself.

Once they set up power in Malacca, the Portuguese undertook expeditions to the Moluccas. In the Moluccas, the two kingdoms ruling most of the spice sources were Ternate and Tidore, the latter rather easygoing in religious matters, but the former bitterly anti-Christian. It is an oddity of history that, in spite of the crusading spirit of the Portuguese, it was with Christianity's enemy, the kingdom of Ternate, that they made a kind of alliance. And it was also there in Ternate that they established their first fortress in the Spice Islands.

Aside from Malacca and the Moluccas, the Portuguese put down few roots, and even in the Moluccas they got into serious trouble. Christian-Muslim enmity made things worse. The famous Catholic missionary, St. Francis Xavier, visited the Spice Islands in the 1540's and missions were established. Many communities went over to Christianity. But, as always in Indonesia, "conversion" could be a matter of power politics rather than belief. A local king with a sharp eye for business or military advantage might find it wise to adopt a new faith. His subjects would swing over with him, though not necessarily changing their customs or beliefs very much, and perhaps swinging back a few years later.

For a time the island of Ambon was both a military and a religious headquarters for the Portuguese in the eastern islands. But at the very moment when rival Europeans were pushing into the area, Portuguese troubles with the local kingdoms reached a crisis. Anti-Portuguese revolts flared up, anti-Christian movements started, and the shaky structure of Portugal's eastern empire began to fall apart.

The final act opened with the treacherous murder in 1570 of a great Indonesian king, Sultan Hairun of Ternate, who had extended his power over a vast area from the Philippines southward. He was slain while under the supposed protection of a safe-conduct. The vengeance sworn against the Portuguese by his son, and the hatred felt by other kings, did much to hasten the end.

Although the Portuguese had been the first to appear in the Indies, in force, other Europeans hastened to join them. Two of Magellan's ships, the *Victoria* and *Trinidad*, touched at Borneo and the Moluccas after the commander's death in the Philippines.

This started an international argument about rights in the Far East. The Pope had made his famous division of the world between Spain and Portugal, and the Portuguese claimed the Indies were all theirs. So the Spanish, hoping to establish their claim, sent a seven-ship fleet the long way around the world—across the Atlantic, around south America, and across the Pacific. Cortez sent an additional group of three ships from his base in Mexico. Only one ship from each group reached the Indies. But in 1571 the Spanish had completed conquest of the nearby Philippines. They were well established there by the time Portuguese power was fading in the Moluccas.

Spain won some posts in the Moluccas, but never became strong elsewhere in Indonesia. However, the ebb and flow of its naval and commercial rivalry with other Europeans at home had a strong effect on the history of the Indies.

Britain and Holland also followed the Portuguese toward the magnet of the Spice Islands. Francis Drake, one of the most famous of British sailors, visited Indonesian waters before the days of his highest glory. He was followed by other Englishmen. British trade developed actively and, as we shall see, much later there was a moment of British political power in the islands. But it was the British defeat of the Spanish Armada in 1588 that played a larger part than any British action in the archipelago itself. With Spanish naval power cut down, the saucy ships of the Dutch could sail the seas with less worry about their former masters.

The way to the Indies was no secret by the end of the sixteenth century. Long before Jamestown and Plymouth had ever seen a white man, Vasco da Gama's route around Africa and Magellan's around South America were well known to Europeans. Ships from various countries had been to the Indies and back, and there was even a kind of guidebook by a Dutchman, Van Linschoten, who had traveled with the Portuguese in the East.

Nowhere was Van Linschoten's book read with more interest than in the seafaring communities of Holland. The first Dutch expedition of four ships left for the Indies in 1595. In the following year they visited Sumatra, Java, and Bali. The next expedition included eight ships, and in the following five years sixty-five vessels made the voyage.

First contacts between the Portuguese and the Dutch were not un- friendly, only suspiciously courteous. But the Portuguese were not keen on sharing the rich prize of the Indies with later arrivals from Europe. A trade war could be foreseen.

A Portuguese war fleet based on Goa and Malacca was ordered to sweep Dutch vessels from the Indian Ocean. But the temptation to attack and plunder other ships also became too strong to resist. The Portuguese came to regard any vessel as their prey, including the ships of the Javanese kingdoms.

The Javanese struck back. They crippled the Portuguese fleet so badly that it was unable to stop the next Dutch expedition when it came. And at the very time when Spanish-Portuguese reinforcements might have been sent to help drive the Dutch away, the British on the other side of the world were blockading the port of Lisbon. Portugal's day was finished, and the future belonged to the Dutch and British, even though Portugal managed to hang onto Malacca for forty years more.

In spite of the bad impression made in some places by the very first Dutch expedition, they were in general welcomed by the Indonesians in the early period. Relations were often friendly, and there were even signs of mutual confidence. For instance, a handful of Dutchmen with a rich store of supplies remained behind in the Moluccas between visits of the fleet. They conducted a peaceful trading business without unhappy incidents, although there was no force to protect them.

The Indonesians thought of the Dutch as allies against Portugal. In any event they liked the chance to play Europeans off against each other in competition for the spices and other articles of trade. If they could have seen into the future they would have been less enthusiastic. The Dutch were to gain a spice-trade monopoly far tighter than the Portuguese had ever dreamed of, and it was often accompanied by cruel hardship for the Moluccas people. The Dutch had started on the road to control of the Indies as a whole.

It must be said, however, that from the beginning of Dutch rule until its end three centuries later, the Dutch were often aided and encouraged by local kings. Many of the local rulers were playing the Dutch game for their own reasons of profit, or to keep up royal dignity, or as part of a power play against a rival kingdom. There was nothing improper in this according to the terms of the day, even though the welfare of the common people had no part in their thinking. The same pattern of colonial history is to be found in many other parts of the world.

Whenever we Americans feel inclined to adopt a high moral tone about seventeenth century events on the opposite side of the world, we should think of examples a little later but much closer to home. The record of the dealings of the white man with the American Indian in the eighteenth and nineteenth centuries leaves little room for indignation against the Dutch at that time, or against local kings who made unwise treaties against their people's interest.

In the rivalry in the East, the Catholic powers of Spain and Portugal were the military enemies opposed by the Protestant Dutch and the Protestant British. But the struggle of lasting importance in the Indies was between these Dutch and British. Or rather, it was between the Dutch East India Company and the British East India Company, both formed to profit from the Indies trade. The two companies were started at about the same time around 1600.

While the Dutch were starting their empire in the Spice Islands, the British concentrated at first in the western part of the Indies. They opened trade relations with Atjeh in northern Sumatra and other pepper producers, and also with Bantam, the kingdom at the western end of Java where the Dutch also were doing business. But the riches of the Spice Islands continued to beckon. The British decided they would like to share in the profitable business of buying cloves, nutmeg, and mace (a by-product made from the nutmeg pod) at low prices in the Indies and selling at fantastic profit in Europe.

England succeeded in taking two small islands in the Moluccas in 1616 (the year of Shakespeare's death), even while expanding their operations in Sumatra and Java. Then, two years later, they sent a fleet of six ships under Thomas Dale, who had just returned from service as deputy governor of Virginia. Dale nearly captured the Dutch fortified post on Java that was later to become the most famous city in Indonesia. This was Sunda Kalapa, or Jacatra. It was re-named Batavia by the Dutch and Djakarta by the Indonesians.

Like British and French generals in North America who had frequent trouble with the Indian tribes allied with them, Dale's dispute with his Indonesian allies cost him dearly. While he and the Indonesian chiefs were arguing about the method of taking what looked like the certain surrender, Dutch reinforcements arrived. The British lost not only Jacatra but, somewhat later, their fleet as well.

Back at home King James I of England had persuaded the British East India Company to make a treaty with the Dutch company. Each was to supply warships for opposing the Spanish and Portuguese, and they were to share both the cost of forts and the spice and pepper trade.

The British company did not really want this plan arranged by their king. They were not keen on fighting in the Far East. Their aim was entirely commercial. The Dutch, though no less eager for profits, wanted to drive all competitors from the area. The partnership did not work, and the British effort at keeping on by themselves had little success. Some British trading posts were continued, but most of their activity was now shifted to India and the New World.

It is interesting for Americans to note that not many years separated two Dutch-British transactions on two sides of the world. Peter Stuyvesant, by surrendering to the British in New York, ended the threat of Dutch competition on the American continent in 1664. And in 1682 the British gave up Bantam, their last important post in the Indies, leaving practically a clear field for the Dutch.

Little by little through the seventeenth century the Dutch gained control over more places in the islands. Sometimes they backed a local king against a rival, sometimes they conquered on their own, sometimes they made trade agreements, but always they kept inching out into wider areas. The British were to have a brief comeback of political power as a distant result of the American Revolution and Napoleonic Wars a century later, and the northern part of the island of Borneo was to come permanently into their sphere. Also, the Portuguese have continued to hold the eastern half of the island of Timor in the extreme southeast. But with those exceptions Indonesia was to be a Dutch domain for three centuries—until the time of the Japanese invasion in 1942 during World War II.

5

Empire of the Dutch

Holland's Golden Age was the seventeenth century. The name is justified by the richness of Dutch cultural life and especially the glory of painters such as Rembrandt and Vermeer and Frans Hals. But it was a golden time of material wealth also.

For that wealth the country owed much to the little band of Dutchmen in Batavia and other Indonesian ports on the other side of the world, as well as to the sturdy seamen who beat their way around Africa and across the Indian Ocean. They were building an empire that was to become almost fifty times the area of the home country, and that was for a long time the mainstay of the Dutch economy.

Life was hard for those colonial pioneers. If this book were about Holland instead of Indonesia, much should be said about the sweltering lives of the Dutch on the frontier of the tropical jungle. There are unhappy tales of cruelty, arrogance, betrayal, and selfishness. But there are also stories of courage, gentleness, and charity. And there is both warmth and pathos in the picture of these people so far from home trying to build a little bit of Holland along the canal banks of Batavia.

Eventually they settled into the country so well that they came to think of it as belonging to them instead of the Indonesians who outnumbered them in the islands 250 to 1. Unlike British colonials who spent their working lives in Asia, but dreamed of plum pudding and shady lanes and British countryside at home, Indonesia *was* home for many of the Dutch. When Indonesia won its freedom, some of the Dutch families had lived in the Indies for a century or so longer than the oldest Anglo-Saxon American family has yet lived west of the Mississippi. Many a Dutchman will tell you with pride that he was born in Batavia or Bandung or Surabaja, and with the same home-town enthusiasm of someone from Amsterdam or The Hague. Bitterness at having lost "his" country to the Indonesians is made more understandable by the touching sentiment of his memories. He is proud—and with good reason—of what the Dutch did toward helping the Indies become productive.

But when we look at Dutch rule from the Indonesian point of view, how different the picture becomes! For much of the time until the twentieth century, and in some ways even until the Dutch finally left the islands, profit for Holland was what mattered. The well-being of the local people seemed to be of little importance.

It is to the great credit of honest Dutch historians that these facts are clearly shown in their own records. And it is to the credit of Dutch humanitarians that they, more than the people of any other nation, deserve Indonesian thanks for first bringing the evils to the light of day, and then working for reform.

Reforms came, but only very slowly, and even those in the twentieth century tended toward close control by foreigners. Little was done to help the individual Indonesian stand on his own feet in human dignity. The Dutch were so absorbed in material progress that they seemed to forget that it is true for Indonesians, quite as much as for Europeans or any other people, that man does not live by bread alone.

The Dutch correctly say that cruelty and tyranny were already in the Indies in home-grown varieties long before Europeans arrived. They merely used existing customs and the oppressive feudal system for their own purposes. Even today an Indonesian servant bringing coffee to a group of his fellow citizens is likely to cringe at the door and remain stooped all the time he is in the room, lest his head be higher than the "masters" whom he is serving. The defenders of Dutch policy point to this, and to other surviving signs, as showing that Indonesians have a natural liking for the master-servant relation and the fatherly guidance of their betters, whether Javanese kings or the bosses of the Dutch East India Company.

The Dutch today, looking at Indonesia's mixed-up political life and the economic disaster that seems to be always just around the corner, say "See! They weren't ready for independence. Everybody would be better off if the Indies were still under our control. Look at what we did for them, and now see the thanks we get!" Indonesians mention the same facts, but in criticism. They feel that much more could have been done in education and in building local leadership during the last century. It should have been possible, they claim, to educate more Indonesians, and to give them more of the direct experience with public affairs upon which a democracy could rest. Many generous-hearted Dutch people said the same thing, but were not able to convince the Dutch government.

Holland's indirect rule through the princes and village headmen, using the old system of oppression and often deliberately strengthening it, seemed to be succeeding. That prevented the Dutch from seeing until too late the great changes going on in Indonesian thought. The new ideas and new spirit burst out, when the time came, in political revolution. But the people had not been prepared, either by education or by going through the steps of self-government, for the heavy task of running their own affairs. The contrast with India's readiness when it broke loose from British control, or of the Philippines when they received their independence from the United States, is very striking.

We will return to this question of independence in another chapter. But first let us follow the steps by which the empire of the Netherlands East Indies was created. Then, in the following chapter, we will note the history-making advances in agriculture and mining brought about largely through the industry and devoted public service of Dutch technicians, scientists, and managers.

Between 1618 and 1621 the Dutch fortified their storehouse at Jacatra, changed the name to Batavia, and turned back the British attempt at taking it from them, as we saw in the last chapter. That may be regarded as the true start of the empire of the Dutch East India Company, in spite of the earlier activities we have described. They went on for three-quarters of a century expanding the field of their operations and pouring a golden stream of profits into the home country.

In 1641 they took Malacca from the Portuguese and defeated Sultan Agung of Mataram who had besieged Batavia. In the 1660's they curbed the wild independence of the kingdom of Atjeh in northern Sumatra (not permanently, however, as the Atjinese make noisy and colorful re-entries into the Indonesian drama every few decades). The last Spanish post was eliminated from the Moluccas, and the powerful kingdoms of Ternate, Tidore, and Makassar were all brought into line.

Shortly after that, the strongest monarchy in Java, that of Mataram, acknowledged the sovereignty of the Dutch. The other leading Javanese kingdom, Bantam, just west of Batavia, was likewise subdued. Through most of the seventeenth century, even after the Netherlands stopped being a great power in Europe, the Dutch position in the Indies was continually strengthened.

Toward the end of the eighteenth century, however, real troubles came as a result of foreign events, though things had been going along fairly well in the Indies themselves. The Dutch had taken a hand in the three long wars of the Java Succession (fights about who would sit on a vacant throne). By the end of the third war, just past mid-century, Batavia rather than any Javanese kingdom was for the first time the major power on the island of Java. The Dutch could—and did—appoint and depose kings at will. Things looked good from Holland's point of view. But misfortunes began to pile up a few decades later, at the time of the American Revolution, when the British blockaded Dutch ports and captured Dutch vessels.

With shipping stopped, unsold goods piled up in the Batavia warehouses, and for a period of about thirty years the colony often seemed on the edge of bankruptcy. It was left pretty much to itself, with little help from home and also without nearly as much direct control as in the past.

When the British fleet stopped the Dutch from carrying goods to Europe, Batavia welcomed the ships of other countries. They made their purchases on the spot and took them home at their own risk. Both Danish and American vessels came often during this period.

But the French Revolution and Napoleonic Wars brought still greater trouble. France conquered the Netherlands in 1795 and upset the old ruling group. A few years later the Dutch East India Company was dissolved, and control of its business was taken over by the new government in Holland. Even before that, however, the British had roundly beaten the company's war fleet in Indies waters.

In 1796 nearly all Dutch territory except Java and the eastern islands was lost to the British. It was given back under the Treaty of Amiens, but within a year yet another war broke out, and once more the Dutch lost most of the islands.

Napoleon put his brother, Louis Bonaparte, on the throne of Holland, and in 1810 formally annexed the country. So the Indies became French territory for a time. If the common man in Indonesia had been aware of what was happening on the world stage, he would surely have felt like a volleyball, being batted back and forth from one country to the other.

The British knew that the colony was weakly defended, and that Napoleon could not send much help to that far corner of his empire. So they moved in with great force, and this time even Java fell to them.

The director of the British attack was the great Lord Minto, governor-general of India. He was a far-sighted imperialist. But he is best remembered in the Far East not for himself but for his brilliant assistant, Thomas S. Raffles, known later as the father of modern Singapore.

Raffles ruled the Indies for more than four years beginning in 1811.

His new idea of colonial government and his deep interest in the life and culture of the Indonesians had a strong influence on later history. Not much was actually achieved during Raffles's own time, but as we look back we see that ideas were planted for the future.

Dutch colonials had always dealt with the princes and nobility. Usually they ignored the culture, religion, and way of life of the people upon whose labor the profit for Europeans depended. Both Raffles and his chief, Lord Minto, however, saw the practical as well as humane need to think of human welfare. Also, they had real curiosity about the history and method of living of these people over whose destiny God (with great wisdom, in their judgment) had placed them. They surrounded themselves with expert students of Indonesian culture and affairs. Raffles himself later wrote a remarkable *History of Java.*

Raffles was ambitious, conceited, stubborn, and tricky. Later he was an intriguer against Dutch-British peace, and some people feel he came close to treason in defying his own government. It is a fact, however, that Raffles was the first European in high authority to put the common people of Indonesia where they belonged—in the center of the picture. For that he deserves an honored place in the country's history, even though he had not done much except make a clean break with the past by the time Indonesia was turned back to the Dutch once more in 1816, after the Congress of Vienna.

Perhaps Raffles's scheme would not have worked anyway, even if he had been given more time, but there was soundness in some of the ideas. He felt that the previous system of "forced deliveries" of produce, imposed on the people through the princes, would not work for the long term. The Dutch officials required a fixed amount of rice or pepper or coffee at fixed prices, and this merely made the princes grind down the peasants. The people doing the real work thus had no stake in the operation and no urge to improve production. Raffles's new plan was based on the theory that a large part of the land belonged to the Europeans in Batavia and could be rented to the peasants, who would thus deal directly with Batavia, rather than with the idle and socially useless kings.

But the village chiefs made the deals with the peasants under this "land rent" system, and they often misused their power as badly as the princes had in the past. There were also other faults in the plan. But it pointed the way toward a more modern economic system and, many years later, the complete end of feudalism. It helped human welfare very little in actual practice, and according to Raffles's many Dutch critics had nothing to do with humanitarian ideas anyway. But it did break entirely new ground in one way. It at least *stated* that the well-being of the common people should be a main objective of colonial management.

About a dozen years after the Dutch had taken back their colony from Raffles came one of the greatest shifts in economic life. This was the "Culture System." Sweeping changes resulted. Under this policy the Indies became, in effect, a huge Dutch plantation, organized and run by the Batavia government. Not only was there more direct control of the individual Indonesian, but the Dutch had a far more active part in the operations. They took charge of selecting crops and deciding how to raise them; they conducted wide research and built engineering works such as the big systems of irrigation.

Before then the Dutch had been chiefly traders, buying produce that the Indonesians were forced to bring to them. Now they were becoming active planters, operating the biggest farm in the world. At an earlier period in the Moluccas they had tried to control production of cloves and nutmeg. But elsewhere, and especially in Batavia, before the Culture System the Dutch had been running trading posts in some ways like those of the Hudson's Bay Company in Canada, or like Bent's Fort and other posts of the Yankee fur traders in the American West.

For some time the new method of active planning and management brought profits. And it brought exciting advances to Indonesian agriculture, as we shall see in the next chapter. The long-suffering peasant, however, had merely gained rule by a foreign country in exchange for the old rule by his own princes. Actually, he was worse off than before, because Dutch control of his life as a farmer did not end the other kinds of tyranny from which he suffered. The king and the village chief kept great power, and this power was sustained by the Dutch as long as it did not interfere with their operations.

Real harm was done to the local "village council," which was a kind of basic democracy. These councils reached decisions by unanimous vote—postponing action until all agreed on a compromise. The headman had been more a spokesman for the group than ruler of the village. But under the Culture System the headman became a virtual dictator because of the economic power given to him by the Dutch.

Some people think that this injury to grass-roots democracy may be partly to blame for some of Indonesia's troubles today. They think that if the village councils had been encouraged they might have laid the ground for a national government, in the same way that New England town meetings gave a solid base for our republic. In any event, the Culture System failed to free the peasant, and it stored up hatreds that appeared in the form of Communism and revolution a century later.

The area under actual Dutch control was greatly enlarged under the Culture System. Or, rather, an actual *area* was now controlled, instead of a few isolated points as in the past. The growth resulted from the new vision of wider inland crop planting instead of relying on trading posts and areas close to the ports.

But it was also a counter move to a swashbuckling British adventurer, James Brooke, later called "the white rajah of Sarawak." In the 1840's he took the northern edge of the island of Borneo, where three territories are still British: Sarawak, Brunei, and North Borneo.

Brooke's Hollywood-style empire-building on one of their own islands made the Dutch see it was high time to confirm their own claims. So in the next fifteen years, inspired both by the British threat and by the chance for profit from new crops, the Netherlands Indies expanded to about the size of the present Indonesian Republic.

During the middle years of the nineteenth century Dutch reformers began to protest against unfair and brutal treatment of Indonesians, especially during forceful "pacifications" in areas newly taken over. From this time on, the government was under constant attack from at least part of public opinion. The officials were accused of breaking treaties, permitting slavery and promoting the opium trade, draining the islands of their wealth without equal benefits to Indonesia, and of treating the people like second-class citizens in their own country. And there was special criticism of the neglect of the educational needs of the people who were Holland's wards.

Just as *Uncle Tom's Cabin* stirred American hearts against slavery in this country, a famous Dutch book, *Max Havelaar,* aroused opinion about Holland's policy in the Indies. The author, Douwes Dekker who wrote under the pen name of "Multatuli," was himself a former colonial official, and he had seen things at firsthand. So had W. R. Van Hoevell, a clergyman who became a strong pleader for more generous and humane treatment after he had been expelled from the Indies for saying the same things there.

People like Dekker, Van Hoevell, and others were supported by a rising tide of European liberalism, and as a result of all these pressures many reforms were carried out sooner or later. Slavery was forbidden in 1860, two years before Lincoln's Emancipation Proclamation. Improvements were made in legal justice. The cruder forms of cheating Indonesians in business deals were forbidden in theory and to some extent actually ended. But the reform that did the most lasting good was the law stopping non-Indonesians from buying land.

In keeping with liberal ideas at the time, there was a big movement of private business into the Indies, and a big immigration from the home country. At first the officials in Batavia had tried to aid their treasury by selling land. There was real danger that, if the policy had kept on, foreign capitalists would have got control not only of the business of the islands but of all the land as well. Ownership would have gone into fewer and fewer hands, making a class of great landowners, and thus leading to the "landlord problem" that still troubles many other parts of Asia.

One of the weak points in recent Communist propaganda in Indonesia has been that they cannot talk very much about "landlordism," which is one of their big arguments elsewhere. Indonesia has many seemingly hopeless problems, but it has at least a solid base of wide holding of land. This trend was carried further in 1961 by President Sukarno's program for limiting the amount of land owned by an individual.

A minor footnote to this is of American interest. The town of Holland, Michigan, owes its existence to the rule about land purchase in Indonesia. A clergyman, Albertus Van Raalte, and a group of his religious followers in Holland had planned founding a colony in Java. When they were ready to leave they learned that they would be forbidden to buy land in Java (though they were offered some in the Moluccas) so they went to America instead. In 1847 they founded the Michigan town that bears the name of their home country and is famous for its tulips.

There were many swings backward and forward through Indonesian history about whether the government should take part in business. The Culture System was merely the most dramatic step. Control of spice production in the Moluccas had ended soon after Raffles. The Culture System put the Batavia officials heavily back into business again, especially with coffee and sugar. It was not until the last third of the nineteenth century that private business began taking over from the officials, and for one crop, coffee, the Culture System did not end until 1917.

The last big change in relations of Holland with its colony came at the start of the present century with the so-called "Ethical Policy." This reflected both the humane influence of reform and a growing feeling among Dutch businessmen that a prosperous Indies could be a wonderful market for what they had to sell. It was also thought that taxes on private business in the Indies would help carry the cost of running the colony. This had become a heavy drain on the home country.

For the Indonesian people the great gain from the Ethical Policy was the new approach to education, public health, and other help to the public welfare. Nationalists later said that these measures were too little and too late, but they did represent a big change from the former official attitude. And some of the Dutch officials in this period, especially some of the teachers and doctors, were as devoted in trying to serve the Indonesians as if they had been working for their own people. They could not get the government to provide the sums they saw were needed, but they themselves did their best.

We know far too little about the life of the common people before the twentieth century. Most of the earlier Western contact was with princes and other highborn people. Few of the Dutch in the Indies studied the lives of ordinary people until quite late in the colonial period.

Before the Culture System, the colonial managers were so out of touch with people away from the ports and palaces that one writer guesses that before 1800 the great majority of Indonesians had never seen a white man. A governor in the seventeenth century boasted that for twenty-five years he had ruled the Indies from his castle in Batavia without ever leaving the town except for one or two hunting expeditions in the jungle nearby. Other stories show that nearly two centuries later many of the Dutch still had little interest in Indonesians or their way of life. Too often there was ignorance of the rich cultural heritage, narrow-minded disgust with the religion, and full certainty that the people were naturally lazy and incapable of education.

The Indonesians' own history does not help us very much, either. It deals largely with royalty and the nobility, and even so reports fanciful events, often just retelling Hindu-Javanese legends in a new setting.

In spite of the lack of full historical sources, we know that control from above had become the natural way of life, whether the ruler was a local sultan, the Dutch East India Company, the Dutch government, or a private corporation. That was a poor background for national independence, let alone democratic life needing a body of self-reliant citizens. It goes far toward explaining many of the troubles the Indonesians have had since winning independence.

6

Nature's Bounty with Man's Help

Whatever judgment history may give about Dutch control of the *people* in the Indies, there can be no question about the wonder, the green miracle, of what they did with nature at the same time. Especially during the period of the Culture System and later, they found new crops and new ways to increase productivity. They also found new mineral deposits and developed ingenious systems of irrigation, transport, and communication.

When Europeans first came to the Indies their frantic interest in quick profits from spices made them overlook a greater prize right under their noses. It was like the fevered gold rush in California in 1849, with little thought at that time of California's far greater and continuing wealth in cotton, wheat, oranges, and so on.

For more than a century after their arrival the Europeans ignored the potential wealth of Java, which since then has become one of the most richly productive spots in the entire world. And the cloves and nutmeg which once seemed like the greatest treasure of the East are now so unimportant in the full picture of Indonesian wealth that we think of them chiefly as part of the closed book of history.

As a matter of fact, the story of the spices in the Moluccas shows the problems man runs into when trying to control production. At the time when cloves and nutmeg could be found nowhere else in the world, the Dutch not only established their monopoly but set about destroying unwanted trees whose produce might have gone onto the market via smugglers, or at least might have lowered the market price by making the spices too plentiful. British, Portuguese, and sometimes American traders were using Makassar in the Celebes as their base, and for a time the smugglers from the Moluccas were busy supplying them.

Destruction of the clove and nutmeg trees in the Moluccas was a tragedy for the people living on those islands. One Dutch historian speaks of them as having been "exterminated" during the forcible conquest, and at all events the natural means of livelihood of many of them was taken away. This control of production (like acreage control and plowing-under in our country at a later day) did keep the price up for a while.

But it would have seemed like poetic justice to the people of the Moluccas if they had known that the policy cost the Dutch dearly later on. World demand for the spices increased, but there were no more trees upon which the Dutch could draw. Although clove and nutmeg trees bear fruit for decades, the first crop does not come for ten or a dozen years after planting. So it was impossible to overcome the shortage soon enough to take advantage of the good market.

In the meantime both the British and French had managed to smuggle saplings into their own colonies. Today, most of the world's cloves come not from Indonesia, but from the islands of Zanzibar and Madagascar, and the biggest nutmeg production is in the British West Indies and Brazil. It is not surprising that after that experience the Dutch decided, in the first quarter of the nineteenth century, that freer trade in spices, without either forced deliveries or restricted production, would be to their advantage.

Forced deliveries were still the rule elsewhere, however, for instance pepper from Bantam and rice from Mataram, the two kingdoms on either side of the main trading base of Batavia. This method of doing business kept on in large degree until the start of the Culture System. In effect, Batavia said to a local king: "We don't care how you do it, but in the next year you must deliver so many tons of pepper, for which we will pay you so much per ton."

The king, wanting the military and financial support of the Dutch, and being prevented by them from trading with anyone else, passed on the orders to his subjects. They were given little help or advice, but simply told the quantity needed. The king, thereupon, returned to his life of pleasures and ceremonies and useless local wars.

At the beginning of the eighteenth century the crops were those that had been customary for many years. Rice was the chief food, and pepper, spices, and sugar brought the largest income. But a spirit of experiment took hold of a few Dutchmen in the Indies, and new ideas were tried out.

Coffee was the first big success. Plants were given to district chiefs near Batavia, and a hundred pounds of coffee beans were produced in 1711. The amount grew and grew to more than ten million pounds a year a decade later. Coffee was Indonesia's chief export crop in the last quarter of the century, and the American slang expression "a cup of java," reminds us of the time when Yankee sailors in the Pacific thought of Batavia as the natural source of the world's coffee.

Coffee was the only big new crop before the Culture System led to wholesale research and experiment. When it did, however, great events followed one after the other. The Botanical Gardens at Bogor, not far from Batavia, became a center of agricultural research. Scientists in many parts of the islands were tireless in trying new plants and new ways of growing them.

After several failures, tea from the Assam province of India was found to be adaptable to Java. A tea garden must have just the right combination of warm temperature, generous rain, and proper altitude, and these conditions are found on Javanese mountainsides. Tea gardens are a most attractive feature of the landscape, and Indonesia is now the third largest tea producer in the world.

Tobacco had come from America, via the Spanish in the seventeenth century, and at least some tobacco was grown from that time on. But it remained for a private company in the nineteenth century to learn how the plant would thrive in cleared jungle districts of northern Sumatra, and how it would respond to the highly scientific method of culture that was adopted. Special types grow in Sumatra, Java, and Madura, each being prized for qualities not found in most other tobaccos.

The oil palm of West Africa was an import to Indonesia in the middle of the nineteenth century, and it proved to be successful almost from the start. Two kinds of oil come from the fruit: palm oil from the pulp, and palm-kernel oil from the pit. The latter is more edible, and is used for making margarine as well as for other purposes. The major use of palm oil is for making soap and candles.

Another picturesque import was the cinchona tree, which came from South America. The new tree took to Indonesian life so well that Java gained more and more of the world market until about ninety per cent of the world's supply of medical quinine (used in treating fever) came from the bark of Indonesian trees. Sales have gone way down in recent years, however, because of use of chemical substitutes.

Kapok, the so-called silk-cotton tree, is another immigrant, probably from South America. The "cotton," which comes from the inside of the seed-pod, is wonderfully useful because of its light weight and because it resists water. This makes it popular not only for upholstery, pillows, and sleeping bags, but also for life jackets. The tree has prospered in other parts of Asia, but nowhere as well as in Indonesia which is the chief supplier to the entire world.

Rubber was the most important of all the new cash crops brought in by the Culture System, although results were so long delayed that it was not until about the time of World War I that rubber came into its own in Indonesia. Before that there had been hit-or-miss gathering of the juice from wild rubber trees in Sumatra. After new Brazilian varieties came in via the Botanical Gardens at Bogor, and after development of the plantation method of production, Indonesia gained its position as the largest producer of natural rubber in the world. In 1959 it fell behind Malaya for the first time, but if general conditions in Indonesia can be improved the country should be able to regain top position.

Sugar, an old inhabitant, responded to new plantation methods, and both the yield and the profits increased greatly. Besides rubber and sugar, other crops most frequently produced on plantations are coffee, tea, tobacco, palm oil, cinchona, cacao (whose beans give us cocoa and chocolate, and whose presence in the Netherlands Indies no doubt led to the fame of Dutch chocolate candy), and sisal for rope and twine.

Some of the important cash crops have stayed in the hands of small farmers from the beginning to the present day. Pepper gardens, which are found most often in Sumatra, are usually small, and frequently are an informal addition to other kinds of work—like the raising of turkeys or sunflower seeds for "pin money" by an American farmer's wife. Until World War II, Indonesia was the largest supplier of pepper, but India now has first place.

Coconut production is almost entirely in the hands of small owners. The product is used in many ways at home and is exported for a variety of purposes by the rest of the world. The export is made in the form of coconut oil or of copra (dried coconut meat). As with so many other crops, production fell off badly during World War II and the aftermath, but Indonesia could still be the world's largest source of coconut oil for soap, margarine, and glycerine, not to mention minor by-products of the tree. These include oil cake, a stock feed made from what is left of the meat after the oil has been pressed out; coir, a fiber made from the husk and used for cordage and matting; and even shredded coconut for American cakes and candy bars.

Even the crops used entirely for home consumption rather than cash sale, and grown entirely by families instead of plantation companies, gained from the scientific advance. The best example is the cassava, a root plant that is even more generous than the potato in producing edible starch. We meet it on our own table in the form of tapioca. The plant had been introduced by the Spanish and Portuguese in the seventeenth century, but better varieties were brought in from Latin America by the nineteenth century scientists. The cassava became, and has continued to be, a food source following only rice and corn as the staff of life for Indonesians.

At first the technicians thought of the forests as their enemy, because crop land was what they were seeking, and the clearing of jungles was a back-breaking job. But before long the wealth of the forests came to interest them greatly, especially because more than two-thirds of all the land area of Indonesia is forested. Many of Indonesia's timber and forest products are used locally, but exports include teakwood, rattan (a climbing palm which, when cut into strips, is a major source of chair seats and wickerwork), bamboo, camphor, barks for tanning leather, and delightfully scented woods whose oil for making perfumes was one of the prized exports to Europe in the early days.

Fisheries also received attention in the scientific revolution, not only studies of the habits of mackerel, tuna, sardines, anchovies, and other fish living in the ocean, but also the stocking of lakes and inland streams, and the development of fish culture in ponds and in the paddies between rice crops.

While some scientists were working along all these lines, geologists, oil drillers, and mining engineers were exploring the mineral riches beneath the earth. Of the products found in this way, petroleum is of course by all odds the most important. Together with tin, it represents a full third of Indonesia's total exports. In world terms Indonesian oil is not terribly important, only about one or two per cent of the total. But the country happens to be the most important source in eastern Asia; and anyway oil can be sold abroad and thus bring money income from other countries. Production in 1959 reached the highest point ever, and this good record is expected to continue for some years before reserves begin to be used up.

Tin had been mined to some extent for centuries, but both its use and ways of getting more of it increased greatly during the age of science. The three small Indonesian islands of Bangka, Billiton, and Singkep, between Sumatra and Borneo, have rich deposits. They give the country second place in the world for amount of tin ore brought out of the ground. And Indonesia is believed to have about a sixth of all the unmined tin in the world.

Other minerals likewise came to light. Bauxite, the aluminum-bearing ore, has become of more importance. Though Indonesia still plays only a small part in world aluminum economy, it is the largest source in Asia outside of the Soviet Union, and bauxite helps Indonesian income through sales abroad. Coal mining was also developed, as well as production of nickel, manganese, salt, iodine, limestone, and a modest continuing amount of two metals that brought Indian seafarers eastward in the first place—gold and silver.

But of all the benefits to Indonesia through the work of scientists, engineers, farm organizers, and managers, perhaps none had more effect on the people than the elaborate irrigation systems. Existing Indonesian systems were improved, and great new ones were designed and built by the Dutch. Especially in Java, these enlarged the area that would bear crops and multiplied the yield per acre of land already farmed. Increase in the total food supply in this and all the other ways permitted a growth in population seeming to defy all the rules of natural limitation.

The island of Java, with its small companion, Madura, had a population of about 5 million a century and a half ago. Today the same area supports—and not badly by Asian standards—about 58 million. There are signs, such as the need to import more rice, that a limit has been reached. And there have been other reasons besides Java's crops for the island's prosperity. Sumatrans, for instance, say that their wealth and that of other Outer Islands has helped to support the Javanese. They complain especially that Java takes too large a share of the money income from foreign sales of oil and rubber produced on the Outer Islands. That is a good point. But the overflowing productivity of Java is still one of the miracles of man's use of nature's bounty.

We spoke earlier of the density of population in Java in general terms, but the facts about Central Java are even more astonishing. The figures according to a 1959 report of the Indonesian government are 1,127 people to the square mile for all of Java-Madura, and 1,337 for the province of Central Java!

All in all, the new approach to Indonesia's natural resources not only brought handsome returns to the foreign capitalists but also gave Indonesia an endowment or "capital plant" that is one of the most remarkable on the face of the earth. Why, then, did the Indonesians want to escape from Dutch management of their affairs that in many ways seemed to be serving them so well? That is another and quite different story that we will come to in the next chapter.

7

On the Road to Independence

When Indonesia declared itself to be a free country in 1945, it passed a historic milestone on a long hard road. It stretched back many years, and to travel it called for heroism and steadfast courage from many people. That milestone, however, was also the start of a much harder path, along which Indonesia is still going. This is the effort at creating a new country and of leading it to a place of honor and dignity among the nations of the world.

We cannot say too often that it seems almost a miracle that there is a Republic of Indonesia at all—so great were the dangers that threatened it on every hand at birth, and so baffling are the problems still faced. But the Indonesians themselves are not content with mere nationhood. They want their country to serve the welfare of all the people, and at the same time to accept its duty as a great free nation in the modern world.

To understand that high challenge, we need to know something of how independence came about, and of how perilously close to failure it has been at many points along the way.

Through the centuries there had been anti-Portuguese, anti-British, anti-Dutch activity, and nowadays these actions might be called anti-imperialist or anti-colonial. But most of them had little to do with personal freedom for Indonesians. Most often a local king was trying to get the upper hand over a rival who was allied with one of the foreign powers from Europe. Those were kings' wars rather than people's wars. Some of them, however, deserve notice in any record of the movement to throw off foreign control.

During the seventeenth century, the Sultan Abulfatah of Bantam, with great energy and cleverness, built a shipping fleet of his own and carried on lively foreign trade with the Philippines, India, and even Persia. He sent ambassadors to other Indonesian kingdoms as far away as the Moluccas, and he invited both England and Turkey to become his allies.

Abulfatah was finally captured by the Dutch and the power of Bantam was destroyed. But a little later a former slave from Bali, named Surapati, caused even more trouble. He was regarded at first as a mere bandit, but he set up an area of his own in East Java. He was joined there by a man familiarly called Sunan Mas, only son of the recently deceased sultan of Mataram. The young sultan held strong anti-Dutch views, so Batavia decided to remove him from the throne. Their troops did that, putting a more manageable relative in his place.

Sunan Mas and Surapati together assembled quite a force in their East Java stronghold. The Dutch had to carry out a long hard campaign before Surapati was killed and Sunan Mas was captured and sent into exile. Surapati was no saint, and in many ways he makes poor material for a national hero. His murder of Dutch ambassadors was painfully like the treachery of Europeans under flag of truce on other occasions. But there was a spirit of "Indonesia for the Indonesians" in his rebellion, and he holds a place among the earlier fighters for freedom.

An even more dramatic rising of Indonesians against the foreigners was led by Diponegoro in the nineteenth century, and it was the biggest until the final struggle. Diponegoro's name is borne today by one of the handsomest streets in Djakarta, and he is regarded by the typical citizen as a freedom fighter who was a century ahead of his time.

Diponegoro was the rightful heir to a throne, and was supposed to be Sultan of Djogjakarta. But Batavia had decided the title should go to a younger brother who they felt was more likely to do their bidding. During the rebellion Diponegoro proved himself to be a cunning guerrilla fighter, and an effective rouser of the people. But he was also a mystic, and that was part of his popular appeal. After he was driven from his throne he spent some time in Hindu-like thinking as a hermit, living in caves and wandering through the countryside. He had wide support from the peasants, who told miraculous stories about him, some of them apparently borrowed from the eleventh century legends of King Airlangga. Before the end many of the aristocrats sided with him also.

For five years Diponegoro carried on his guerrilla war. It was a tragic campaign in which deaths from cholera and famine were far more than those on the battlefield. Diponegoro must have been a careless reader of the history of the Indies if he was surprised at what happened when he finally accepted a Dutch invitation to come to their camp to talk about surrender. He was promptly arrested and sent into exile!

This Diponegoro revolt began over a familiar dispute about a throne, but it grew into a popular struggle. It was a real predecessor of later fights for freedom, in that sense perhaps like Bacon's Rebellion in Virginia a century before the American Revolution.

There were other examples of standing up to the foreigners, including some under the leadership of warrior queens. But special mention must be made of Atjeh, where a rugged and unquenchable people live at the northern tip of Sumatra. From the beginning of Indonesian history right to the present day, they have shown a rambunctious spirit that reminds Americans of Texas under the Lone Star flag. No one has been able to keep the Atjinese down for long.

Atjeh has had its relatively quiet periods, but it keeps bursting out all over again. Its position on the Strait of Malacca made piracy convenient, and the Atjinese took to it with joy. They resisted the kind of "pacification" that the Dutch found rather easy to apply at other places in the islands. Their longest fight with the Dutch began in 1873 and lasted for over thirty years. Their guerrilla bands have been a thorn in the side of the Republic in recent years, and only time will tell whether the peace signed in 1959 will last. Atjeh has not typified the peaceful spirit of co-operation needed for a democracy, but through the centuries they have shown a fiery spirit that suggests one side of the national movement.

As the world moved into the twentieth century, and as profits for foreign investors soared to heights never known before, it became clear that Indonesians would refuse to go on forever with little voice in their own affairs. And it was also clear that if they had a voice they would try to divert more of the profits into education, public health, better living conditions, and other welfare purposes.

In an American study of the income per person in fifty-three countries at the end of the Dutch period, just before World War II, Indonesia was Number 53 with an average of $22 per year! In a largely agricultural country such as Indonesia it is not easy to keep track of all the income in the form of food both raised and eaten at home. Even so, Indonesia's place at the bottom of the list in spite of the wealth it had given to Holland through the years was deeply resented by the nationalists. And of course the Communists made full use of the fact in their propaganda.

Most Indonesians had passed the point where they would accept anything less than real self-government. They were bitter against the halfway measures by which they felt the Dutch were putting off the inevitable day when Indonesians would take things into their own hands. The most serious fault of the Dutch in the twentieth century was that, right up to the moment of independence and even afterwards, they were unable to believe that the freedom movement was real.

The national spirit had been growing like a flood that begins with tiny streams in the distant hills, gradually swelling into a mighty river. The officials thought of the nationalists as mere "trouble-makers" who could be put down with a strong hand. And they felt that any Dutch who favored self-government for the Indies were little more than traitors. But the spirit of independence was becoming ever stronger. Events elsewhere in Asia encouraged this.

The Japanese victory in the Russo-Japanese War in 1905 proved that Asians *could* defeat Westerners. And the earth-shaking Chinese Revolution in 1911 showed how an Asian people could take destiny into their own hands and throw off an outworn system.

Many other strong tides came from abroad. In fact the Indonesian freedom movement seems to have spread out most strongly from just those parts of the country having greatest contact with the outside world. The three biggest influences from abroad, each greatly modified in Indonesia, as was always the case, were a European idea of social justice; the new movement in Islam that tried to combine social and political reform with religion; and international Communism.

One of the first groups contributing to a national spirit in purely Indonesian terms was Budi Utomo ("Lofty Endeavor"), organized in 1908 by three medical students to encourage interest in Javanese culture. One of the three, Sutomo, was an important leader in the freedom movement later on, but the society itself was too long-haired for mass support. It was useful, however, in putting down local roots for the movement that in so many other ways drew inspiration from abroad.

Social democracy of the sort known in Europe appealed at first to dissatisfied Dutch and to Eurasians and Chinese. Through them radical social ideas came to the Indies. One of the biggest questions within the independence movement was whether freedom and democracy could be gained without falling into the trap of Communism.

Religion was a leading force in preventing the Communists from reaching their goal, which was to capture the national movement. Of a group of Muslim organizations the most important was one called Sarekat Islam, which was strongly influenced by the "modernist"

Muslims of the Near East. They had a new vitality in their attitude toward religion, and at the same time they were working for political and social reform. The Sarekat Islam was the extreme eastern end of this movement, and they were determined to keep themselves Islamic, Indonesian, and non-Communist.

One of the leaders of the Sarekat Islam was Hadji Agus Salim ("hadji" showing that he had made the holy pilgrimage to Mecca). He was one of the chief intellectuals in the freedom movement, and later was foreign minister of the Republic. In one of the showdown struggles to keep out the Communists, the Hadji said they had no monopoly on advanced ideas. He pointed out that Mohammed, the holy prophet of Islam, had been preaching socialist economics twelve centuries before Karl Marx was born!

But although the Communists were turned back from their try at seizing this particular society, they made progress elsewhere. By the middle of the 1920's an underground movement existed, though, oddly enough, at first without much encouragement from Moscow. A Communist uprising in 1926 was actually against the Kremlin's ideas. Lenin and other Russian leaders had not expected success for Communism in so-called backward countries. The Moscow bosses of world Communism kept brushing off the over-eager party organizers in the Indies. Later the Soviets decided they had been wrong, and both they and the Chinese Communists have come to think of Indonesia as an important area for their work. Communism very nearly got possession of the revolution at one of its most critical moments, and the Communist Party in Indonesia has grown enormously in membership and influence since independence.

But the New World played its part also. We must give a high place on the list of foreign influences to the ideas of the Rights of Man that had been expressed by the leaders of the American Revolution and then restated in other ways in the French Revolution.

When the revolutionary French overthrew the ruling group in Holland, and brought in the new ideas of liberty, equality, and fraternity, the colonial officials in Batavia wrote home in some alarm to ask if anything of that sort was intended for the Indies. They were told to relax, that the new doctrine was all right for Europe but naturally not for backward Indonesia.

Dangerous thoughts kept coming in, in spite of Batavia's efforts. One finds among most educated Indonesians a deep respect for our founding fathers, and especially for people such as Jefferson who gave noble expression to the very thoughts for which they themselves were reaching.

The national spirit centered in Java, which was the richest island, the most populous, and the most open to ideas from abroad. But movements for both independence and social democracy occurred on the Outer Islands also, especially Sumatra. The idea of bringing all the parts together, however, was slow in coming, and many Indonesians as well as the Dutch thought it would never happen. It was curious that two foreign enemies—Holland and Japan—must be credited with helping to bring it about.

The unity of the Dutch system within their colony is perhaps the most basic reason for the existence of the Republic of Indonesia to-day. If the Indonesians had been left entirely on their own, without a central Dutch system, it is quite possible that the different islands might have kept on going their separate ways in spite of their general cultural unity.

The Dutch did what they could to prevent *Indonesian* unity—for instance, even forbidding use of the word "Indonesia" and from time to time banning use of the growing national language. But they could not do their job as colonial managers without their own kind of unity which later was taken over by the Indonesians.

But if Holland laid the groundwork, the Japanese fixed the timing. The Japanese invasion of the Indies in 1942 and other events of World War II speeded up the coming of unity and freedom. If it had not been for the Japanese, many Dutch think Holland would have been able to work out some scheme of self-government within a Dutch system like the British Commonwealth. They had started very late, however. Even if the reformers had had a free hand they might not have been able to make up the time they had let slip while British India, for instance, was getting ready for its freedom.

As World War II developed, however, German occupation of Holland, beginning in 1940; Japanese occupation of the Indies; and the commitment of all countries in the Atlantic Charter and Declaration by the United Nations made it certain that the old order of things would not be resumed after the war. The great question was whether *some* form of Dutch control would be imposed once more, or whether Indonesia would become entirely free—if, indeed, Communism did not smother freedom as well as capitalist imperialism.

At the start of World War II, some of the Indonesian nationalists felt that an Asian alliance of some kind would give them their chance to break the Dutch hold. These people said they had no concern with events in Europe.

Others saw that Hitlerism was a threat to freedom everywhere. They put their faith in the principles of the Atlantic Charter signed by President Roosevelt and Prime Minister Churchill, and later by other countries including Holland. Even the growing signs that Japan, the major Asian power, would come in on the side of Germany did not stop them from supporting the war against Hitler. They were anti-Dutch, but not anti-Allies.

When, even before Pearl Harbor and American entry into the war, the Japanese began moving south toward the oil, rubber, tin, and foodstuffs of Southeast Asia, it was clear that an invasion was coming. And it was just as clear that the small forces of the Allies would not be able to stop the Japanese. Furthermore there was an ancient legend that a people who sounded rather like the Japanese would someday come to clear foreign invaders from Indonesian soil.

The invasion came in 1942. The Japanese quickly overran the islands, captured or drove out the Dutch and other Allied forces and took full control of the Indies. The Japanese immediately pretended to have great enthusiasm for the idea of Indonesian independence. They said they had come to rescue the poor islanders from the cruel rule of Europeans. The Indonesians had some true grievances, as we have seen, so the Japanese propaganda had great effect. Societies and military units were formed under Japanese sponsorship, with flowery statements of purpose with which an Indonesian patriot would naturally agree.

Many Indonesians saw through the trick at once and refused to have anything to do with these organizations. But many others did participate, some for selfish reasons, some because they were fooled, and some because they thought it was a way of helping the cause of eventual freedom.

Among the last were two of the most famous of all Indonesians, Sukarno and Hatta, who later became president and vice-president of the Republic.

These particular "collaborators" acted deliberately, and by agreement among several of the most prominent leaders of the revolution. Some would be outward "collaborators" with the Japanese, some would run a secret underground movement, and some would take to the hills and organize guerrilla bands in time-honored Indonesian fashion.

As in the resistance movements in Europe during the German occupation, the Communists in Indonesia played a full and useful part side by side with anti-Communists for much of the time. It was only later on that interest in serving world Communism rather than Indonesian freedom became the clear goal. Until then it seemed that the first thing was to get rid of the Japanese, the next was to prevent return of the Dutch, and the last would be to decide what kind of government the new country wanted to have. For the moment, differing long-range views were suppressed.

Little by little it became clear that the Japanese purpose was imperial rule and the placing of Indonesia in a bondage worse than anything the Dutch had ever dreamed of. Although the Japanese were fellow-Asians, and even fitted the ancient legend about the yellow-skinned rescuers, Indonesia realized long before the end of the war that life in a Japanese puppet state would be even less attractive than under former Dutch rule.

As the end of the war neared, the Japanese tried to make things look better by offering Indonesian "independence," but a strong group of nationalists was opposed to accepting anything as a gift from an invading army. There was a big argument among the leaders, and at one point Sukarno and Hatta were kidnapped to prevent them from putting out a statement disapproved by the others. At last most of the groups agreed, and Sukarno read Indonesia's own brief declaration of independence on August 17, 1945. Loyal Indonesians barricaded themselves in radio and telegraph offices to send the message to all parts of the country.

The Republic of Indonesia had begun its career. The question now was whether it could live very long among the many perils that threatened it. The Dutch wanted to get their colony back, the Communists wanted to take control of the revolution for their purposes, and nobody knew whether the different regions could really unite into one country.

8

The Fight for Freedom

To declare independence is one thing. Actually to secure it is something very different—as both Americans and Indonesians know from the history of their fights for freedom. President Sukarno's declaration in 1945 was the start of a heroic struggle that was to last more than four years before true independence was won.

The Dutch naturally wanted to go back to running their colony again just as quickly as possible. They thought that America, Britain, and their other allies in the war against Germany and Japan should help them. The Communists, meanwhile, talked independence but actually wanted to enslave the country to their party under the leadership of the Soviet Union. And, as if that were not enough enemies for one young republic, Indonesians differed with each other about the future of the new country. Some were true patriots but disagreed about methods. Others were seeking personal power or had some other special interest.

While the Japanese controlled the islands, Indonesian guerrillas and the underground resistance had been planning an uprising timed for the expected Allied invasion. When word came that, because of the atomic bombs, the Japanese had given in to the Allies under General MacArthur in August, 1945, months sooner than had been expected, the Indonesians moved to disarm the troops in the islands.

But the Allied high command did not realize the strength of the independence movement. They told the Japanese troops in the Indies to keep their arms, maintain order, and await arrival of Allied forces before surrendering. This was hard for the Indonesians to understand, after waiting so long, but worse was to come.

British troops came in first. They were welcome enough in themselves, but then Dutch soldiers began arriving under their protection. The Dutch demanded arrest of Sukarno and tried to persuade their allies that the so-called independence movement was just a Japanese plot and the Indonesian leaders puppets and traitors.

Tragic events followed, especially in heavy fighting in Surabaja, where the nationalist government was not able to control semi-organized bands who ran wild. Atrocities were committed by both sides.

After much argument and some action, an Indo-Dutch truce was signed in November, 1946. This was followed by an agreement for a "United States of Indonesia" in which the Republic of Indonesia would be one of the states. The other states in this federal system were Dutch-organized governments from other parts of the islands. According to the Republic people, this was merely a scheme for the old-time "indirect rule" in new form. In the next few months there were many arguments about how the agreement should be carried out. In July, 1947 the Dutch launched a full-scale military attack on the Republic's territory.

Through the good offices of the United Nations this military action was ended in January, 1948, but with the Republic's territory reduced to a portion of Java and a little bit of Sumatra. The Republican capital was in Djogjakarta, while the Dutch held Batavia.

A few months later the Communists chose to start a rebellion *within* the Republic. The Republic's leaders were busy indeed, putting

down the Communist rebels with one hand and trying to hold the
Dutch to the agreed truce line with the other.

With the Republic hemmed into its small area, and with the Dutch
actively organizing the other parts of the Indies, it looked once more
as if the Indonesian nation had reached the end of the road. Dis-
cussions about the truce agreement finally came to a deadlock, and
in December, 1948, Dutch paratroopers fell upon the Republican capital, while troop carriers brought in commandos.

President Sukarno and other top leaders were captured. The chief
cities of Java were seized. Yet once again it seemed like the final
curtain. But still the Indonesians would not give in.

Besides Sukarno, the leaders who were led into captivity after they
had been seized in Djogjakarta included Hatta, Sjahrir, and Hadji
Agus Salim. Who were these people, and what were they like? This
is perhaps a good time to give a few facts about these men whose hold
on the people was so strong that, even in exile, they were the heart
of the revolution.

President Sukarno has had a justified reputation as one of the greatest charmers of the modern world. He has always been perfectly
dressed, carrying an air of strength and "bounce," and with a winning
smile. As a public speaker he has had an almost mystic power to sway
a crowd. He was born to be a master-of-ceremonies. With zip and
energy he has accepted any chance to be an organizer—whether of
a mass meeting, a songfest, an impromptu folk dance, or a national
revolution. Although president of the Republic, he has gloried in the
name Bung Karno, "bung" meaning brother and being a word used
to summon waiters and for other purposes something like our "Hey
Mac!" It became a symbol of equality during the revolution.

During his longest visit to the United States in 1956 his pleasing
personality won friends everywhere. He made a special pilgrimage
to Monticello because of his deep admiration for Jefferson. When a
collection of Jefferson's writings was published in Indonesian trans-

lation a few years ago, Sukarno's remarks about Jefferson during his Virginia visit served as the introduction to the book.

Sukarno was educated as an engineer and he is therefore sometimes referred to as Ir. Sukarno, that is Engineer Sukarno. But his true profession has been leadership. A first name, Achmed, is often used by Westerners who cannot get used to the Indonesian custom of normally going by only one name, but to most of his fellow countrymen he is just Bung Karno.

His enemies say he has been a demagogue, a seeker after power through appeals to the masses. His admirers think he has truly expressed the ideas and hopes of the people. His following, in any event, has been among the mass of the people rather than among Westernized intellectuals, many of whom were unhappy about his recent acceptance of Communist support.

Whatever the results of Sukarno's later policies, it must never be forgotten that he is the man, more than anyone else, who welded the country together, led it through the trials of the revolution, beat the Communist rebels and the Dutch imperialists, and kept Indonesia an independent country.

Mohammed Hatta, a scholarly type of person, logical in his thinking, and with a strong appeal to intellectuals, was Sukarno's long-time partner in revolution. He was an excellent teammate for Sukarno, and together they are the most basic heroes of the independence movement. While Hatta was a university student in Holland, he helped organize an Indonesian independence society. After Sukarno was arrested by the Dutch, Hatta went back to the Indies in 1932 and took over direction of that part of the freedom movement that later proved to be its head and heart. Two years later he was himself arrested, and he was held for eight years, first at a jungle outpost in New Guinea and later on one of the Banda Islands.

Hatta and Sukarno were so closely linked during the revolution and the early years of the Republic that the expression "Sukarno-Hatta" was used as if for a single person. It was natural for Hatta to have, at different times, the titles of vice-president and prime minister, and for him to have been the key factor in national policy at many tense moments. He resigned as vice-president in 1956, and he criticized Sukarno publicly in recent years on a number of issues. The break between these two great leaders was a matter of sadness to many Indonesians.

Sutan Sjahrir, another of the leaders arrested when the Dutch paratroopers dropped on Djogjakarta in 1948, was a longtime companion of Hatta in imprisonment and exile. He also had been a university student in Holland, and he returned home when Hatta did. His moving and fascinating letters to his Dutch wife, published in English translation in America under the title *Out of Exile,* show the depth of the intellectual and spiritual experience through which the two men passed. They seem to have read at that time nearly everything from the Bible to Marx and Freud.

At the last moment, just before the Japanese invasion, the Dutch realized that Indonesian patriots such as Hatta and Sjahrir might be helpful in the defense. They arranged to have an American flying boat, one of the last Catalinas away from the Dutch base at Ambon, make its escape by way of the Banda Islands, pick up Hatta and Sjahrir, and bring them to Java.

Sjahrir was prime minister three times, a key negotiator with the Dutch, and the most important of all Indonesians in telling their story to the world when he came to present their case to the United Nations in New York.

Sjahrir's acceptance of Sukarno's patriotic motives in his prominent collaboration with the Japanese during the war was convincing, for Sjahrir himself chose the dangerous course of the secret underground. He had his own organization that he directed while traveling around Java or posing as a laborer on a relative's place. He was in touch with other groups, including the Communists. He had secret meetings with Hatta, so that both the collaborators and the resistance knew what the others were doing.

Hadji Agus Salim died in 1954. He was the grand old man of Indonesian independence. Although he was a devout Muslim who had made the holy pilgrimage seven times, he was alert to every modern trend in world scholarship. He lectured at several American universities, and to many people in the world he was "Mr. Indonesia." He combined modernism and piety in his attitude toward Islam and helped protect the Islamic branch of the independence movement from capture by Communism. With his tiny frame and wizened merry face, he represented a spirit and integrity that are treasured by all Indonesians. He was several times foreign minister and a perfect representative of his country before the world.

While these men were being held by the Dutch, the revolution was bravely continued by others. An emergency government was set up in Sumatra, out of Dutch reach, and the fighting in Java was carried on heroically under General Sudirman who, though a dying man, kept on leading the troops, even after he had become so ill that he had to be carried from place to place.

Each time the Dutch proposed a new truce, the Indonesians said that Sukarno and the others must be released first, and the Republican capital must be moved back to Djogjakarta. The United Nations commission, which had been appointed earlier, now became newly active. Concessions were made by the Indonesians, sometimes under urging by America. Although Holland blames America for our support to Indonesia during the struggle, the Indonesians think that, because we did not understand conditions in the Indies, we often accepted Dutch arguments too easily and pressed the Republic to give in on points where they should have stood firm.

American public opinion was strongly with the Republic from the start. But our State Department was concerned with the defense of Europe against both Russian military threats and possible Communist takeover of weak European governments. Our government did not want to do anything in the Indies that would weaken Holland at home. But the Indonesians and their friends in the United States said that the many thousands of troops and hundreds of millions of dollars that Holland was using in trying to reconquer the Indies might better be used in Europe. They pointed out that the money Holland spent on military actions in the Indies was about equal to the total it was getting from America under the Marshall Plan.

As the facts became better known in America there were public demands, including some in the U.S. Senate, that we give the Dutch no more help at home until they had stopped fighting the Indonesians or at least had pulled back to the agreed truce line.

Meanwhile Asian countries that had never before taken an important part in world affairs made clear their support for Indonesia. And the Soviet Union, always glad to get into the act posing as a friend of Asian peoples, gave its strong support also.

Finally, as a result of the many pressures, the Republican leaders were released and returned to Djogjakarta, and an Indo-Dutch conference was held at The Hague. There, on November 2, 1949, an agreement was signed recognizing the Republic of Indonesia as the sovereign power in all the former Dutch East Indies except New Guinea, which was left for later discussion. The two countries were to be in an Indo-Dutch Union under the symbolic leadership of the Queen in somewhat the same way that free and sovereign Australia and Canada are members of the British Commonwealth. Some years later even this tie was cut, and Indonesia stood alone as one of the entirely free nations of the world.

On December 27, sovereignty was turned over to the Indonesians in Batavia, which was immediately rechristened and known after that as Djakarta, a modern form of its old Javanese name.

The man representing the Republic at this ceremony was one of the most interesting of modern Indonesians. This was the Sultan of Djogjakarta, whose royal name is Hamengku Buwono IX. His loyal public service has enabled him to become a national hero in spite of republican prejudice against royalty.

Although the Sultan is a descendant of a long line of Javanese kings and was brought up in the tradition of absolute rule (subject only to approval by the Dutch!), he has proved himself to be a good democrat. While certain other members of the royalty were scheming with the Dutch to betray the revolution as a way of getting back their former thrones, the Sultan of Djogjakarta boldly threw in his lot with the Republic. He refused any discussion with the Dutch except on the subject of when they were going to get out.

During the Dutch military action the Sultan was a colonel in Indonesia's national army, and later he served as minister of defense in one cabinet and deputy prime minister in another. He has special interest in the problems of youth, and one of his positions is as chief scout of the Boy Scout movement.

The great achievement of the nationalists under Sukarno was to bring together all the kinds of Indonesians—from every island and every way of life—into a whole. The peasant from a remote district was now a citizen of the Republic along with the Sultan.

One of the interesting trends was the bringing of women prominently into public life. They played a full part, often a courageous and heroic one, in the freedom movement. In the years since independence women have become more and more important in the life of the Republic.

One able woman, Mrs. Maria Ulfah Santoso, was minister of social affairs in an early cabinet, and thus probably the first woman cabinet member in any Muslim country. In later years she served as executive assistant to one prime minister after another, although they came from different political parties. She has often been a real key to the functioning of the Indonesian government.

Quite a number of women have had seats in the national parliament, membership on UN delegations, and other positions. In all government departments you can find offices directed by women at least as frequently as in our government.

In spite of the success of the Republic in winning the loyal support of many kinds of people who had never worked together before, there were sections of the population not playing a loyal and orderly part in the common life.

We saw earlier that the religion of Islam was a force helping to hold the country together, at the same time that modernist Islamic ideas aided the movement for social justice. But there were, and still are, extreme Muslim groups, especially in the organization known as Dar ul-Islam. They believe in the use of terrorism and violence in trying to change the Republic into a completely religious state. They have defied civil authority, they dominate the countryside in the areas where they are strong, and some of the guerrilla bands have continued to hold out for years, especially in northern Sumatra, Borneo, Celebes, and the mountains of West Java.

The Communists were in decline for a while after their unsuccessful rebellion in 1948, and the party bosses confused their followers by dazzling shifts of the "party line." In recent years, however, and especially as there has been growing public discontent because of flaws in the government, there was a great gain in Communist Party membership. Furthermore, President Sukarno seemed to encourage them by his "neutralism" and his effort at walking a political tightrope. Like a number of other Asian leaders, he wanted to keep out of the cold war between the U.S.A. and U.S.S.R., and at the same time to have the support and friendship of both major powers.

A more or less neutral foreign policy is undoubtedly approved by the majority of Indonesians, even by many of those who are strong anti-Communists. They want Indonesia to be loyal to itself rather than to any foreign country.

But some of the President's other policies created deep controversy in the country, especially his plan for "guided democracy." Under "guided democracy" there is no fully representative government as we know it in the West; parties are restricted, there are curbs on freedom of speech and of the press.

The Communists supported this plan. President Sukarno's defenders think that, in spite of that, his policy was the only one to prevent the Communists from getting control of the government.

In money matters Indonesia has been in serious trouble. The Japanese occupation was followed by a "scorched earth" policy used in fighting against the Dutch in parts of Java and Sumatra, and the Dutch blockade of Republican territory was of course itself harmful. Production of both food and the sources of foreign income (rubber, oil, etc.) naturally went down. Then came the difficult period of getting the new Republic started, followed by one in which poorly trained Indonesians tried to take the place of Dutch specialists who withdrew or were expelled as a result of squabbling between the two countries. Many Indonesians thought it was unwise to seize Dutch businesses before there were enough trained local people able to run them.

On top of everything came a time in which Indonesians saw that bribery and dishonesty (from which they thought they were freeing themselves when they took control of their own affairs) were still found in many parts of their own national government.

Because the central government was in Java, and the most active crooks and black marketeers operated in the capital city of Djakarta, people in some of the Outer Islands, and especially in Sumatra, began to express anti-Java ideas with more and more violence.

Finally, in 1958, a full-dress rebellion was launched in Sumatra. It was led by men who had given important service to the Republic in the past—governor of the Bank of Indonesia, dean of the university, leader of one of the chief political parties. It looked once more as if the Republic of Indonesia was beginning to fall apart.

But, as so constantly in the past, Indonesia had surprises for the world. The government, and especially the army, moved with speed and efficiency. Even though some army units joined the rebels, the uprising was put down quickly, the leaders took to the hills or fled to Singapore and Hong Kong, and the authority of the central government was established once more.

The part played by the army in this and other dramatic events in the years since independence should be noted carefully. Under the vigorous and attractive chief of staff, General Nasution, a pious Muslim, the army served as a kind of balance wheel in Indonesian political life. Many people think that the army's religious and democratic influence is what prevented the Communists from taking over the country during several recent crises.

Through all of the troubles—war, revolution, occupation, famine, corruption, and the threat of Communist domination—the incredible Indonesian people have shown courage, resilience, patience, and hope.

Two Indonesian principles of great age continue to play a part in the life of the country. One is the idea of "gotong rojong," or mutual assistance. This principle is vitally alive. In spite of the hard struggle to get enough to eat, it is said, "A village might starve, but not an individual alone." That is, mutual assistance assures some sharing of both good and bad fortune.

The other basic idea is "musjawarah," or discussion. Because this does not mean quite the same thing in Indonesia that it does with us, Western visitors sometimes find this term maddening. To an impatient man musjawarah can be misunderstood as "talking all the time without ever doing anything."

Some foreigners seem to think these things are shortcomings in Indonesian life. It is possible, however, that the traditions of gotong rojong and musjawarah give a basis for Indonesian democracy. It might be quite different from ours in its methods and yet could be faithful to those ideas of Jefferson that President Sukarno himself helped to popularize in Indonesia.

9

The People

Physically the Indonesians are among the most attractive people on earth. There are unhandsome individuals among them, of course, but mostly they have well-formed features, perfectly turned limbs, and sturdy but graceful bodies. Most Indonesian girls seem to be remarkably pretty.

They tend to be a short people. In photos of international groups, the tops of the Indonesians' heads are often at about shoulder level with the Americans. Some Indonesians are quite a bit taller than the average, and there is a theory that Javanese royalty and nobility, having had closer connections with India in Hindu-Javanese times, are naturally taller—"more kingly." They are said to have "kraton stature," that is, proper for a palace. But the proportions of the people of more normal height seem so perfect that there is no reason why they should want to be taller.

The skins are brown, varying in darkness from area to area. In the capital city of Djakarta, where there are people from all sections of the country, you see almost every shade. Many Indonesians have a facial appearance that Americans often speak of, carelessly and inaccurately, as "Chinese." There are actual Chinese in Indonesia, but they have tended to keep racially and culturally apart. The "oriental" appearance of the true Indonesians traces back, rather, to the old Mongoloid elements in the Malay people who invaded all of Southeast Asia. Because of the common racial heritage, an American is often unable to guess whether a given person is from Malaya, Indonesia, or the Philippines.

Quite properly for the citizens of a new country, the people look young. Many of the leading figures actually *are* young because poor education or no education kept down the number of educated people in the older generation. But there is an appearance of youth and freshness anyway. President Sukarno has never looked his years (his birth date is usually given as 1902), and in many pictures General Nasution has looked more like an eagle scout than the chief of staff of a national army.

Not only are the people good looking, but they have a natural grace that is shown by laborers at heavy tasks as well as by delicate dancing maidens. And they have courtesy, poise, and incredible patience.

The Indonesians have continued about their daily work without violence during many incidents in the last dozen years that would have caused positive explosions in many other countries. Patience and musjawarah—the habit of discussing things—may often serve in Indonesia as a substitute for the rioting one might expect in the same circumstances in some other countries.

The position of Indonesian women may have something to do with this—or may merely reflect it. Women have a higher, more useful, and more important place in Indonesia than in most countries of Asia, and certainly more than in any other Muslim country.

One of the pioneers chiefly responsible for helping Indonesian women to come out into the world was a little Javanese princess named Kartini who died in 1904 at the age of twenty-five. Even in that short life she started a revolution. She was one of the most charming and spiritually minded of all cultural heroines. She wanted, for herself and other Indonesian women, the right to play an active part in the world's work, freed from the restrictions of tradition and Islamic customs. She was practical in what she did, but one of the most typical sentences from Kartini is "I want to make myself worthy of the highest title, and that is a Child of God."

With the devoted help of Dutch friends, she acquired a good education. Then she started a school for girls, and later started another one in her new home when she married a prince of Rembang.

Kartini's letters were published in Dutch in 1911, and the book became the basis of the women's movement in Indonesia. It appeared in English in an American edition in 1920 under the title *Letters of a Javanese Princess*. A girls' school was started in Kartini's memory in 1912, and her birthday, April 21, is observed each year as Kartini Day throughout the country. As an Indonesian woman journalist wrote in 1960, "Through her, Indonesian women saw the light."

The first building to be erected as a school for girls was the project of another princess, Dewi Sartika, a West Java pioneer in urging freedom and education for women. More schools grew from this, and Dewi Sartika inspired others to follow her example.

We spoke in the last chapter of women who have held important offices. But useful work by women is not limited to government jobs. In journalism, education, library work, medicine, social work, law, accountancy, and many other fields, women have proved to be Indonesia's "secret national resource." Even in business one finds the same thing. A study of the batik industry in the city of Djogjakarta in 1957 showed that half of all the firms in that business were run by husband and wife jointly, and a quarter were run by women alone. Indonesia is making very intelligent use of its woman-power.

The condition of religion, as well as the position of women, reflects the tolerant spirit. Although more than nine-tenths of the people are Muslim, the Hindu and Christian minorities are in general well treated. As a matter of fact, because the Christian tribes had better education from missionaries than the colonial government was giving to the people generally, there is a relatively high percentage of educated Christians among old people. These people, and especially the Bataks from Sumatra, have played a useful part in the government of the Republic. Christians hold a higher proportion of important government jobs than we might expect from their tiny percentage in the total population.

Indonesian Muslims are set apart from the rest of Islam in various ways. Foreigners—even including some visiting Muslims from other countries—are sometimes fooled into thinking that "Indonesians don't take religion very seriously." That is a wrong idea, based on surface signs. These include the fact that Indonesian women have not worn veils; that the mosques, the places of worship, are not impressive compared with those in other Muslim countries; that the Minangkabau people still have "matrilinear" families, that is, tracing the line through the mother instead of the father; that everywhere Muslim law is mixed with customary local law; and that not many Indonesians have more than one wife, even though Muslim law theoretically permits four. But Indonesian Muslims are for the most part loyal and devout, and many thousands of them make the holy pilgrimage to Mecca each year. Islam is intensely important not only in Indonesians' personal lives—in their feeling of direct relationship with God—but also in public affairs.

Islam, like Christianity, is a daughter of Judaism, the historic religion of the Jews. These three faiths are called "monotheistic," that is, believing in one God. They have so much in common that an American finds it easy to understand many of the main ideas of Islam. The word "Islam" means submission (to the will of God), and a "Muslim" is one who submits. Jesus is deeply revered, and many of what we think of as Christian virtues might also be called Islamic virtues.

Just as the teachings of Jesus have, at different times in our own history, been a force for social reform, Islamic ideals have helped lead the way to change in Indonesia. Muslim parties have figured largely in the political life of the Republic, as well as in the fight for independence, the movement for social justice, and the attack on spiritual emptiness, whether of Communism or Western materialism.

One of the great successes of Sukarno and the other leaders was to combine the religious and non-religious groups into one powerful national movement strong enough to beat the Dutch and keep the Communists from taking control. But after independence had been won and the Dutch troops had departed, it became difficult to hold the groups together. Just as the Communists had tried to "run away with the revolution" for their purposes, some religious groups tried to seize control for *their* own reasons.

As we said before, the fanatical Dar ul-Islam is in actual rebellion against the government and using terror to rule the sections it controls. It is as violent in trying to impose an Islamic state as the Communists are in trying to establish the kind of government they want.

It must be understood, however, that the *stated aims* of both groups —so different from each other but sometimes so alike in method— have wide support from Indonesians in general. The ideal state described by the Prophet Mohammed in seventh-century Arabia has a great appeal for many twentieth-century Indonesian Muslims. And the ideals of social and economic justice that the Communists say they are following are naturally attractive to people exploited through long centuries by their own princes as well as by foreign invaders.

Without wide education and knowledge of what has happened under Communism in other countries, the simple Indonesian peasant or the city worker without property has a hard time believing the warnings that non-Communists give him. Only when Communists gain some measure of control and then fail to bring any improvement in the life of the individual citizen is it possible to judge claims against actual results.

Muslim groups have been the Communists' chief opponents. In the recent past the political party called Masjumi was the largest, and until it was ordered to disband in 1960, it was regarded as the strongest anti-Communist force. Another Muslim party called N.U., much closer to the grass roots, joined the Communists in supporting certain government policies; but it also is believed to be an anti-

Communist force of great strength. And the basically Muslim spirit of the army is believed to be the reason for the generally non-Communist position it has taken in recent years. Islam is important in every phase of Indonesian life—not just on Friday (their holy day) but every minute of every day.

But we have learned by now that nothing in Indonesia ever turns out to be just what we might have expected. The country's incredible ability to absorb and adapt and modify everything it gets from abroad applies in the field of religion as well as everywhere else. Beneath Islam are those layers of Hinduism and Buddhism and animism from still earlier eras. Even after all the centuries that have now passed since the Koran was brought to the Indies, old beliefs keep cropping up and old folk customs are intertwined with Islamic ritual.

Just for example, the Islamic rule against idols is so strict that in some Muslim countries a picture of a human being is considered immoral. There have been cases in which cartoon figures on factory safety posters were forbidden. That is an extreme example, but even in some highly modernized Muslim countries a picture of a religious figure is so shocking that pages have sometimes been torn out of Western books in libraries in order to remove the offense. Yet in Indonesia some Muslims among the common people, without any feeling that they are doing anything wrong, bring offerings to the great Hindu statue of Lara Djonggrang (Slender Maiden) in Central Java. The same sort of thing goes on in other parts of the country, with offerings to other statues, as well as to stones, graves, and trees.

The folklore of the peasants and the stories relating to their many festivals and ceremonies are filled with the special local brand of Hinduism, even in sections that have been completely Muslim for centuries.

There are even Hindu legends that have been adapted to point out Islamic morals, or to provide the framework for purely Islamic stories. In the dramas, and especially in the puppet shows which we come to in a later chapter, the stories are of Hindu origin, though with adaptations to make them apply to Indonesian history and folklore in a Muslim society.

But, because Indonesian culture is so complex, even Hinduism does not tell the whole story. Lying beneath everything else is the ancient animism or belief in spirits and ancestor worship going back to times even before the Hindus came.

Folkways whose origins are lost in the mists of centuries are still active forces in the life of Indonesia. The word that scholars use for the putting together of ideas from varied sources is "syncretism." For us it is enough to say that the Indonesians are absolute masters at taking a little here and a little there, molding them together, adding a touch of something left over from a few centuries earlier, and ending up with something never before seen on earth.

The same sort of drawing from many sources has occurred in every other field besides religion. Many of the economic ideas come from the old forms of village life, but there are also bits from the Dutch Culture System as well as typical capitalism of the Western world. Ideas of social reform have come from nineteenth century social democracy and twentieth century thoughts about the welfare state. Business is often based on methods from Europe, America, India, and China. Political thoughts have been taken from Jefferson, Marx, Roosevelt, Gandhi, Sun Yat-sen, Kemal Atatürk, Mao Tse-tung. Manners and social customs are based on teachings from a wide variety of sources—from the legends of King Airlangga to the lively present-day instruction of Marilyn Monroe and Pat Boone.

Because Indonesian society, and the ideas of the Indonesian people, are made up in this unusual way, we must expect that solution of the country's problems may be unique also. Their way may be quite different from ours, yet the best for them.

10

How They Live

We were talking, at the end of the last chapter, about the most important things in any country—the people and what is going on in their minds and hearts. That is hard to describe directly, but sometimes we can get useful hints from outward signs. Let us take a look at houses, clothes, food, and the customs relating to them in Indonesia.

There is one similarity among almost all Indonesian houses, whether the design is old or new, and whether the people living there are primitive or very modern. Side walls are not very important. What really matters is the roof. That is natural in a country where the weather is always warm, but where heavy rain can always be expected.

As a matter of fact, some houses, and even many public buildings, have virtually no side walls at all, but only screens of bamboo or palm matting that can be put in place for shading or for protection against a driving rain. Some houses do have heavy walls, which may be planks in some rural areas or masonry in Dutch-type houses in the cities, but even those usually have big doors and windows to give an open effect. And decorated porches are used as living space and become important features of many buildings.

The main dining rooms of leading hotels are often entirely open to the outside air on two or three sides, and this is so in most public restaurants except the very rare place that is air-conditioned.

The all-important roofs in Indonesia are made of nearly everything you might think of—slabs of wood used like shingles, thatched palm fiber, and lots of tile, usually red or salmon colored. In the modernized cities red tiles are almost standard, but you also see them in country areas, even though everything else about the house is flimsy.

Much of the "personality" and special character of the houses come from those wonderful roofs. The most picturesque are the palm-thatched roofs of the Minangkabau people in Sumatra. Their houses with richly decorated sides are regular museum pieces, especially if seen as a backdrop for colorful groups of people in local costumes. But the crowning glory of these fascinating buildings is the series of delightful upward-swooping roof-points. The small rice barns, always near the houses, are miniatures in the same charming style. There are few forms of home architecture in the world more naturally pleasing to the eye than the Minangkabau houses.

In Madura there are splendid "buffalo horns" at the ends of the ridgepole, the Batak and Dayak people have their own special forms of roof, and in Djakarta the red tiles above white walls lost in greenery make Americans think of Florida or southern California.

Wood carving, often gaily painted, has been one of the traditional arts in Indonesia for centuries, and there is some kind of carving in almost all the different varieties of houses. Carving is seen on pillars, rooftops, sidewalls, or porch ceilings. In some of the communities, especially in Borneo, there are carved wooden figures at the entrance to the living space to scare off demons. Carvings of Hindu figures or symbols are important in all Balinese villages.

In many areas the majority of the houses are raised on stilts a few feet above the ground, and the entrance may be a short ladder or kind of gangplank. The raised position keeps snakes and other wild things from running in and out, it lifts the building out of the mud, and it allows better circulation of air.

An oddity of Indonesian houses from our point of view is that "apartment houses" are found in the country but there are scarcely any in the cities. In the poorer sections of the cities—slums, as we would say—people are jammed together tightly in hovels. But better city housing is usually intended for single families, mostly all on one floor and pleasantly landscaped. Just recently a few handsome apartment houses have been put up in Djakarta, but in general the good residential areas in even the largest cities tend to have a peaceful small-town air about them.

In contrast, the back country is where multi-family houses are found in great number, and in some areas that is the normal way of living. There may be separate structures, grouped in a kind of "clan" community of related families, as in Bali. The Minangkabau houses that we have discussed gain a new wing each time a daughter is married. In Borneo the tribes have wonderfully complex long-houses, sometimes with rooms for a hundred or more families. They have been compared to the former long-houses of the Iroquois in New York State or to the pueblo villages of the Zunis in the American Southwest. In any event, the closeness of family relationships is clearly shown in the housing tradition of nearly all sections outside the cities.

Like the pueblo Indians with their "kiva" for the ceremonies of each group living together, the Hindu people of Bali have a little family temple or shrine within each compound, though there are village temples as well as the famous larger ones. In the Muslim communities on other islands there are village mosques, but each large house normally has an assembly room for ceremonies, festivals at certain times of year, coming-of-age celebrations for young people, and even the puppet shows we shall meet in the next chapter.

Warm weather naturally affects clothing as well as houses, and the garments are proper for the climate. Indonesian men, like their brothers everywhere, tend to leave the fancier forms of dress to the ladies, except on special occasions, such as the brilliant ceremonies at the "kratons" (palaces) when *everybody* puts on gorgeous costumes. Then the scene is in full Technicolor. But on normal days the men in cities who are government officials, businessmen, office workers, etc., dress very much as Western men would in a hot climate.

In less formal jobs, where an American might wear slacks and an aloha shirt in the summertime, the Indonesian may have a handsome shirt of batik, the special fabric we shall describe later, that gives much the same effect. Indonesian office workers have become so attached to Western appearances that some people with perfect eyesight have been accused of wearing horn-rim spectacles with plain glass, just for looks, and of carrying brief cases with nothing in them but a noonday lunch!

City workers in lower positions may go bare above the waist or wear white or colored or khaki Western-style shirts with open neck and short sleeves. These shirts, by the way, are usually remarkably clean, even when worn by manual laborers, in spite of the fact that there may be few washing facilities except a filthy canal. Below the waist they wear either white or khaki shorts or the famous wraparound skirt called a "sarong." And the sarong is found in almost all country districts as a normal garment for men as well as women.

All the white-collar people in the cities wear shoes, but laborers, restaurant waiters, and house servants do not. Outside the cities most of the millions of people have never had their feet in shoes. Even prosperous people enjoy barefoot relaxation in their handsome city houses or mountain cottages, and they also often wear sarongs at home, much as American men may wear slacks or shorts on week ends, even though dressing formally during the working week.

The one article of clothing for men that can be seen everywhere is the black velvet cap called a "pitji," which has become almost a symbol of national unity. You see it worn by anyone from the president of the Republic to the lowliest peasant.

Except for sarongs and occasional batik shirts, there is not, normally, a great deal of color in men's dress, but the ladies more than make up for it!

A sarong or a cloth called "kain" (material) is the essential base of the costume, but decorations and accessories of many kinds give exciting bright accents. A cloth of another color worn over the shoulder is attractive in itself, but can also be used as a shawl over the head, for carrying parcels or babies, or for various other purposes. Some women holding professional jobs in the cities now wear Western-style sleeveless dresses to the office, but even they always put on the brilliant national costume for parties and public occasions.

Hair is drawn into a tight bun and decorated with tiaras, pins, clasps, combs, etc., made of shell, silver, gold, painted wood, and other gay materials. Flowers in the hair are frequent additions to the charm of the headdress. As a matter of fact, the Indonesians like to use flowers, singly or in the form of leis, on all occasions. In the famous Madura bull races, the animals themselves are decked with garlands.

For festive wear Indonesian women wear magnificent jackets made of rich brocade. They also have gold-painted sandals made of wood, and handsome costume jewelry.

Cotton is the most widely used cloth. It may be a cheap mass-produced print or a luxurious handmade batik. There are sections of the country, out of touch with the cities, where clothing is of "tapa," a fibrous material made by soaking and beating the bark of certain trees. And there are still primitive areas left in which ideas of what the well-dressed man or woman will wear go back so many centuries that a loincloth made of leaves is the principal garment.

Umbrellas and parasols are used more for protection from the sun than from the rain. An attractive do-it-yourself umbrella frequently seen along the roadway is a banana leaf, picked up on the spur of the moment and held over the head. As in many Asian countries, the few common people who own shoes often take them off and carry them in their hands when the road is muddy. A little mud will not hurt bare feet, but it could ruin a pair of shoes that had cost more than a month's income.

Transport is a special problem in this country of islands, mountains, jungles, and swamps. Not much railway trackage is found outside

Java. Interisland boats are much more important. On land the system of roads, though far from complete, does connect main centers. In spite of improvement in highways and in the number of trucks in the country, the human body is still the chief means of transport.

Men, and especially women, carry enormous loads on their heads. This is supposed to be the reason for the fine straight posture, and also for the habit of holding the head still and turning only the eyes when looking up or down or to one side.

The most common of all roadside sights in Indonesia is a porter with heavy loads (fruit, rice, coconuts, or something else) at the two ends of a long "balancing pole" across his bare shoulders. To control the jouncing of the load with each step, the porter has a special humping gait to reduce the up-and-down motion of the pole. It looks like the strange "heel-and-toe" pace used in Olympic walking races.

There are few taxis in the cities, and their place is filled by a bi- cycle-rickshaw called a "betjak." At one time there were said to be eighty thousand of these in Djakarta alone. A jolly feature of the betjak is the sound made by a rubber band usually stretched be- neath the rickshaw part of the vehicle, while the driver peddles the cycle behind. The rubber band whirs in the wind as the betjak wheels along. The loudness of the note varies with the speed of the vehicle; this gives the peddler and his passenger a feeling of progress, and it also helps warn people on foot that they are about to be run down. In some cities the taxi service is provided by the kind of horse-drawn cart that the British call a dogcart, and that the Indonesians have therefore named a "dokkar." It is pulled by a sturdy relative of the small wild horse from Central Asia.

Besides horses, the most numerous domestic animals are water buffalo, cattle, chickens, goats, pigs, sheep, cats, and dogs. The enor- mous water buffalo, the carabao, is a descendant of the wild ox, and has horns often measuring six feet across. The chickens, however, are almost all very small, which seems right because the kind of hen that we call bantam came originally from Bantam in western Java.

Because good Muslims do not eat pork, pigs are found most often in the Hindu and Christian areas.

Primitive tribes that depend on hunting for their meat use spears, bows and arrows, blowguns with poison darts, and various kinds of traps. Their game includes deer, pheasant-like birds, monkeys, and wild boar. A traveler among the Kubu people in Sumatra not many years ago reported that they would eat "almost anything from decayed elephants to grubs and worms."

But outside of the hunting tribes Indonesians are not great meat-eaters. Rice is the staff of life in much of the country. Picturesque terraces marching up the hillsides, and the paddies on the plains, are typical features of the landscape in Java, Bali, southern Sumatra, and southern Celebes. This "wet-rice" culture of the richest part of the country is marvelously productive, and gives two or three crops a year. Where the soil is less good or water not available, or at all events where man has not come to the aid of nature in the same way, the "dry-rice" method is used.

Without irrigation there is a much poorer yield. The dry method is also called "burn and plant," and that is a good description. You clear and burn an area of jungle, plant the crop over and over again until the land is worn out after a dozen years or so, and then move on to a new patch.

The wet-rice system is interesting in a number of ways besides the main question of food supply. For one thing, it was the wet-rice system that brought prosperity to certain areas, making possible a high state of culture and the civilized refinement of such arts as dance and music. It also helped develop engineering skills and scientific planning for the irrigation system of dams, ditches, bamboo aqueducts, and water elevators powered by the flowing water itself.

But the greatest effect of the irrigated method of growing rice is that it teaches fair play, tolerance, and co-operation. It is a kind of primary school for democracy. An individual peasant could not afford to build a whole irrigation system just for his one small plot. But by teamwork a group of neighbors can do it together. And, having done it, they cannot help learning about joint management of their project. The spirit of "live and let live" is found wherever there is sharing of water for the rice fields.

Thieving birds will eat up an entire rice crop if you let them, so much effort goes into driving them away. Little windmills that whir as they turn may be set up among the paddies, or a child may be posted to shout and clap his hands. But most interesting of all is a co-operative system that, like irrigation, teaches the idea of helping one another.

A platform on stilts is set up in the middle of a wide group of rice paddies, and overhead strings lead to it from all the fields, some of them hundreds of feet away. One guardian of the crop can watch the whole area and, by pulling the proper string, create a disturbance in the field that is being invaded. Owners of the different fields take turns supplying a boy for the job.

In the eastern islands generally, and in parts of Borneo and elsewhere, sago takes the place of rice as the chief food. The sago palm has a spongy center rich in starch. The tree is cut down, this central pith is cooked, and we can say that people in the sago area quite literally live on trees!

Even in the rice areas an additional food of great value is the cassava, the source of tapioca. As we noted in Chapter 6, it came originally from South America. Its rootstock has even more starch than a potato, and it is cooked according to many local methods, some of which produce a paste something like the famous "poi," which our own Hawaiians make from taro root. In acreage planted, the cassava comes next after rice and corn. One of the good things about cassava is that it grows fairly well in soil much too poor for rice.

Yams, soybeans, eggplant, and peanuts are among other important food crops. Peanuts figure in festive meals in a way that is new to us. Bits of meat are broiled on skewers, like shish kebab but tiny in size, and are coated with chopped peanuts. Indonesia is one of the few places where you are likely to get the flavor of meat and of peanut butter in the same mouthful.

For all these crops, the work is done by hand labor and by primitive plows pulled by buffaloes or oxen. The handmade iron hoe called a "patjol" is the most usual hand tool. The fields are too small for tractors, and anyway foreign machinery is much too expensive and hand labor very cheap. Tractors are used to a limited extent on some of the big plantations growing cash crops.

Coconuts are both a major food source and a cash crop for export. Most of the cooking oil used in Indonesia is pressed from the coconut meat.

Fish are abundant and becoming more so with development of both ocean fishing and the inland fish culture. Among the most unusual ways of life in the whole country is that of the "sea gypsies." These are fishing people who literally spend their lives in their small boats, not like dwellers in shore-tied houseboats so frequently seen elsewhere in Asia, but true seafarers who keep to the open ocean a great deal of the time, even during furious storms.

Of all the good things to eat that grow in Indonesia, nothing pleases the foreign visitor more than the plentiful fruit. Perhaps the most frequently seen is the papaya that seems to grow with the speed of light. It develops from a seed to a twelve-foot tree bearing fruit in seven or eight months. Bananas are in dozens of varieties and sizes and flavors. Some of them are twice as big as any we can buy in this country. Pineapples are abundant. More unusual fruit include the jackfruit, the mangosteen, the rambutan (looking like a sea anemone), the mango, and the durian. The last two deserve special mention.

Almost everyone agrees that mangoes are among the most delicious fruit in the world, but there is hot controversy as to how you should eat them without ruining your clothes. The edible part clings to the large flat pit, and the fruit is extremely juicy. This difficult combination has led to the invention of many different methods. The only really dependable one is to put on a bathing suit and proceed directly from the dining table to the bath.

The durian is an evil-smelling fruit, yet it has a wonderful flavor.

An English traveler described the smell as "sweet drains" (British slang for a sweet-smelling sewer), but one American fancier wrote that the durian tastes like pineapple ice with crushed cashew nuts.

As in all of Asia, there is not enough food to go around. The Indonesians are better fed than much of India and some other underfed areas, but there is a constant race between the food supply and the rapidly growing population. Whatever affects the crops is a matter of life and death to the people. It is not surprising, therefore, that religious functions and folk festivals are connected with the planting season, the growing season, the harvest season, and the warding off at all times of evil spirits.

Such festivals are colorful affairs, and they take many different forms, but almost all involving music, dancing, drama, and the finest costumes the village can produce. There are ceremonies of many other sorts during the year also, marking every stage of man's life from birth to death. Some of these are peculiar to small areas, others are quite similar on different islands. Some of the occasions, such as the Madura bull races, have become internationally famous in the same way that the snake dances of our Navaho Indians, at first a purely local custom, have become known around the world.

Wedding ceremonies illustrate the principle of "Unity in Diversity," for although they are quite different from each other in many ways, a foreigner can see similarities among the different Muslim areas, and even likenesses between those and the functions of the Hindus on Bali and the Christians in the Moluccas. The one common element in the varied cultures of all the islands is a love of music, drama, and the dance. We will examine that richest field of Indonesian art in the next chapter.

11

Music, Dance, Drama, and the Arts

Music, dance, and theater—but theater of a very special sort, as we shall see—are among the oldest as well as the greatest glories of Indonesian culture. Most of us in the Western world have just begun to learn about them. They are so different from the forms we know that they seem very strange at first.

For some centuries most Europeans who went to the Indies thought that the music they heard there was crazy, most of the dances boring, and the dramas of a kind that no one would understand. Also, the all-night performances were so tiring that the weary foreigner usually just gave up.

But, little by little, careful Dutch, German, English, and American students have unfolded to us the unsuspected wonders of these Indonesian arts. And, thanks to traveling companies of dancers and their orchestras in our own country from time to time, we can sometimes see and hear for ourselves. Our progress in understanding is suggested by the fact that a summer course in Indonesian music was started at Harvard University in 1960.

97

Actually, the very first report on these arts in the English language was favorable, even though little improvement in understanding was made for some centuries after that. When that old sea dog, Sir Francis Drake, visited the Indies in 1580, he had his ship's musicians entertain a local king. The compliment was returned when the king had *his* orchestra perform. Drake recorded that he had heard this king's "country-musick which, though it were of a very strange kind, yet the sound was pleasant and delightful."

If Drake had gone on to talk about the instruments making the pleasant sounds, we should probably find out that they were about like those in use today, almost four centuries later. We know that in many parts of the Indies there has been little change, though elsewhere there has been influence from region to region, and some from abroad.

The Republic is now trying to get Indonesians to learn about the arts and crafts of the entire country. Even today, however, certain instruments and certain kinds of music are heard only in some of the islands. Dance and drama, as well as music, are the most developed in Java and Bali or at least have been the most carefully studied by people from the West.

The most usual kind of Indonesian orchestra is called a "gamelan," and it has a big part to play not only in dances and dramas but also in the constant festivals and ceremonies we mentioned at the end of the last chapter.

"Gamelan" means hammer, and that is a good name for the orchestra, as most of the instruments are beaten or struck. A musician might say that a gamelan is chiefly the percussion section of an orchestra. The basic instruments are gongs, drums, and what might be called xylophones. There is a stringed instrument with one, two, or three strings played with a bow. And there is a wood wind, a kind of flute. The human voice, either solo or in chorus, is also frequently used.

In some sections of the country there are fascinating additions to the list of instruments, though these are often played in other combinations rather than in gamelan orchestras. These instruments are different from anything we have seen in the West, but they might be said to belong to the general families of the tambourine, rattle, cymbals, chimes, oboe, lute, violin, zither, bagpipe, and jew's-harp.

In Celebes there is a marching flute-and-drum corps (no drum majorettes, however). Especially in West Java and Sumatra there is a kind of bamboo hand-xylophone called a "shake-angklung" which is very popular in schools and with youth groups. Each instrument has a fixed tone, and the person holding the angklung gives it a shake each time the music calls for that note to be sounded. This gives good training in teamwork without need for much knowledge of music, and a school in Princeton, N. J., recently started an angklung orchestra for that reason.

The gamelan instruments are beautiful to the eye as well as the ear. Highest craftsmanship goes into the working of the metal and wood, and the frames are usually gorgeously decorated. Often the instruments do not belong to the individual but to the village, palace, society, or some special group.

Many gamelan collections are very old and are famous in themselves. Perhaps the best known is the great Holy Gamelan in the royal palace at Djogjakarta. Some of these instruments are enormous in size. Legend reports that the Holy Gamelan goes way back to the time of the Madjapahit Empire. It has been adopted by Islam, however, and now plays only once a year, on an anniversary of the Prophet Mohammed.

Whether or not the particular instruments are of a known age, their form can be clearly traced back for centuries, and in some cases to a time even before the coming of the Hindus. But the palaces of the Hindu-Javanese kings were the greatest centers of a highly developed musical life. We are reminded of court composers and court orchestras in Europe at the time of Bach and Handel.

The intricate music played by the gamelan is not written down. It is passed from teacher to student through one generation after another. That was one of the things that troubled the early Europeans. Those rough-and-ready merchants and adventurers, seeing that there were no written notes, and being themselves unable to hear anything that sounded like a melody in the strange scales, decided it was just noise instead of music.

We have an advantage over them in two ways. One is that we are more tolerant of other cultures, less certain that our way of doing something is the only right way. But in addition, the music we hear in the West today has moved a little closer to the Indonesian variety.

Claude Debussy's whole-tone scale, which we no longer find too difficult to accept, is said to have been suggested to him by a Javanese gamelan that he heard at a world's fair in Paris.

Composing the music and arranging it for an orchestra may follow a method something like that of a modern combo's jam session in America. That is, the composer-arranger gives ideas on his own instrument, while the others follow his lead, but make inventions and new contributions of their own.

In Java there are two scales, both of which normally have five tones. Readers who know music might be interested in a few details about them. One of the scales, called "slendro," has notes that are something like D, E, F sharp, A, B. The other one, called "pelog," has more uneven intervals, going something like D, E flat, F, A, B flat. Sometimes one or two more notes are added; and for singing smaller intervals are also used.

The gongs have special meaning in dividing the musical phrases. Gongs of different size and tone indicate the ends of large or small sections of the melodic line.

In the Christian sections of Celebes and the Moluccas, hymns and other Western music became known fairly early. And in various parts of the country there is now growing interest in our music, both classical and popular. President Sukarno, a great enthusiast for both singing and dancing, is reported to have sung for visitors a selection of American songs. The stirring national anthem, "Indonesia Raja," is in a Western scale.

There are even cases in which a Western theme is combined with the Indonesian themes of a gamelan. Modern popular songs are written in Western scale, and are often heard on the radio. And the shake-angklung we mentioned above has been adapted to our scale. Groups of young people in Bandung and Djakarta can be heard lustily singing such tunes as "My Bonnie Lies Over the Ocean" and "Home on the Range" with angklung accompaniment.

More and more Indonesians have gained a taste for our symphonic or operatic music while studying abroad, and our dance music is familiar to large numbers through radio and movies. But these are still only a fraction of the people on every island and of every station in life who know and deeply love their own music.

The dancing with which gamelan music is connected is really a form of drama. There *are* folk dances, and the general population takes part in these. But the best known Javanese and Balinese dances and many of the others are performed by specially trained people for an audience. Usually they tell a story.

Each gesture has definite meaning for the onlookers. Westerners seeing Indonesian dancing for the first time appreciate the graceful movements, but are usually surprised to discover that legs and feet are the least important parts of the body for these beautiful movements. Often, in fact, the dancer may be seated or squatting down for much of the dance. The arms, fingers, head, and neck do most of the dancing.

Westerners find it almost impossible to copy the motions exactly, even after years of practice. For instance, the apparently simple gesture of forming a *perfect* circle with thumb and forefinger, and snapping it open and closed, is something nobody from the West has ever been able to do to the satisfaction of an Indonesian.

The best dancers begin their training as children, and in some areas, such as Bali, the girl dancers usually stop performing when they enter their teens. There is always a spirit of youth and freshness, as well as incredible grace and precision, in this age-old Indonesian art.

Nearly all the dances except the folk dances require special costumes, and these are often of great brilliance and richness. Elaborate masks are also worn for some of the performances, and there are often stage properties such as fans, flowers, parasols, lighted candles, saucers, and the wonderful ceremonial sword or dagger called a "kris."

The plot or scenario of each dance is known to the audience. That does not spoil their enjoyment. On the contrary they like to "know how the story is going to turn out." They anticipate each gesture, and they know the inner meaning of every movement of head or arm.

As we would expect from other things we have learned about the country, some of the stories are from ancient folk legends, but many had their origin in the great books of India, though changed to the new conditions in Indonesia. Some, also, deal with current events, especially the fighting against the Dutch during the revolution.

Americans do not take puppet shows very seriously. At least we would not think of a Punch-and-Judy as a natural way of presenting religious ideas. But puppets seem to Indonesians to be one of the highest forms of dramatic art. And they are absolutely tireless in watching the shows that they love so much. A typical performance begins at 9:00 P.M. and ends at 6:00 A.M.

Puppets are of different kinds, but all are called "wajang." The word means shadow, and the most familiar sort uses silhouettes held up to a screen lighted from behind. But there are other kinds of puppets in three dimensions; and one sort of full-scale drama with human actors is called "wajang-orang" because orang means man. The reference to shadows in all these forms of theater, even if they are not shadow plays, is explained by the Indonesians in a beautiful way. They say that a drama is a shadow of life, and that man is a puppet of God. There is a moving poetic prayer, "O Lord, make me a wajang in thy hand," that is close in spirit to the Book of Psalms.

The popularity of wajang shows the final proof—if any were needed by this time—of local influence on foreign ideas, even if they are as strong as the religion of Islam. As we noted in a previous chapter, representations of the human figure are supposed to be forbidden in Islam. Yet here are the pious Indonesian people giving their enthusiastic approval not merely to pictures but to figures in the round. The flat grotesque puppets, which are the most popular in Java, may have been a Muslim substitute for the more lifelike figures used before the coming of Islam. This possibility is suggested by the fact that in Hindu Bali the earlier type continued without a break.

The most popular form of shadow play is called "wajang-kulit." The figures are flat cutouts made of buffalo hide, stiffened with a gluelike substance, and magnificently painted in gold and other colors. Each has a horn handle. They are works of art in themselves. In some parts of Indonesia the men in the audience sit behind the screen, so they can see the actual puppets, while the women and children are out front and watch the shadows on the screen.

For the screen, a white cloth is stretched on a bamboo frame with a light behind it. This can be an electric light in a city, but much more frequently it is a coconut-oil lamp. At the bottom of the screen, lying horizontally, are two soft trunks of banana trees into which the puppet handles can be stuck. The gamelan orchestra, which is part of every wajang show, is also behind the screen.

Our American expression "as busy as a one-armed paper hanger" is a fair way of describing the activity of the conductor of the wajang show. He is called the "dalang." He must be—all at the same time —the speaker of the story, the handler of the puppets, the conductor of the orchestra, and the creator of special sound-effects. He sits at the bottom of the screen, and holds up the flat puppets so their shadows are on the sheet. Because so many of the puppets represent noble or royal figures they must never be disrespectfully placed below the dalang's head.

At one side of the dalang is the orchestra and at the other his chest of equipment, holding not only the collection of puppets but also noisemakers of bamboo and metal.

The stories though impossibly long for an American viewer, and including bits of history and legend that are strange, use general

themes that are not a bit unusual for those of us who go to neighbor-
hood theaters or drive-in movies. Some of the characters are different
(demons, etc.) and there are mystic swords and sacred figures not
found in our movies. But the struggle is still between the good guys
and the bad guys (the good ones usually winning), or sometimes the
effort of the boy to get the girl.

Even the plays having deep religious meaning, and given on religious occasions, have a lively quality of exciting popular drama. The
puppets have a strong hold on the public interest, whether shown in
a permanent theater in a city such as Bandung or by a traveling
dalang who goes into the farthest parts of the back country.

The flat puppets are of great artistry, but those in three dimensions
are even finer examples of the talent for carving, molding, and deco-
rating. They have the same craftsmanship shown in other Indonesian
arts that have come down through the ages.

We have already mentioned the skill of Indonesian wood carvers
in connection with the houses, and every American visitor to Bali is
likely to bring home one of the elongated carved figures for which
the island is famous. So, too, with pottery and metalwork of many
kinds. Silver filigree as delicate as a spiderweb is a specialty of some
sections, and the glasses, pitchers, and bowls in solid tin are so
tastefully designed that they are often used on fine tables in place
of silver.

In an earlier time the highest level of art was reached in the design
of arms and armor, especially the kris. This small sword or dagger
was originally an actual weapon, but has now become a symbol. Even
today there are art collectors who regard a perfect kris as one of
the most beautiful objects to be seen in Indonesia. The workman-
ship of the metal blade is only the beginning. The handle and scab-
bard have the same splendor of design.

Even in the field of toys and casual playthings for children, Indonesian artistry is shown. Beautiful and entertaining toys are made
from paper, bamboo, clay, wax, banana leaves and stems, coconut

shells, palm leaves, and other simple materials. There is an endless variety of play hats, parasols, kites, wriggling "snakes," rattles, and other noisemakers. American children visiting in Indonesia have been known to abandon their own expensive mechanical toys and turn with joy to these attractive examples of Indonesian folk art.

But of all Indonesian handicrafts the best known both at home and abroad is the fabric dyed by the method called batik. Nowadays there is a great deal of mechanical or semi-mechanical printing of cloth, but the ancient method of making hand-batik is still used.

Melted beeswax is applied to the cloth from a little pitcher of a special shape. The wax is put on in lines according to the design that has been planned ahead of time. Then, when the waxed cloth is dipped in the dyeing vat, the color "takes" only on the unwaxed portions. After the first dyeing, the wax is scraped away, a new design is applied in wax, a new color of dye is used for the dipping, and so on until the full design is finished in all its colors. The job is so difficult that two months are frequently needed for good work, and as many as six months may be given to batiking a sarong of special quality.

There is some use of the "tie-and-dye" method used by American home dyers, but it may be a more delicate operation than we normally see here. The Indonesians sometimes tie tiny thread-ends in a careful pattern, rather than whole sections of the cloth.

We noted, when talking about houses, the great skill and sense of design in the painting of wood. As far as design is concerned, the making of batik is quite similar to that. But formal painting on canvas is an art that was slow in developing. This is rather surprising because the Dutch came to Indonesia in considerable numbers during the Golden Age of Dutch painting, and are even said to have brought occasional Rembrandts and Vermeers with them. However, the painting of canvas had not been important in the Indies, and there was such slight cultural contact with the Europeans that painting as an art form (as opposed to the decoration of objects and buildings) did not get its real start until quite modern times.

Now, however, there are lively groups of Indonesian painters and sculptors, and there is a famous collection of their work in the president's mansion in Djakarta.

Many Indonesians, and foreigners too, fear that imports from the West, or local copies using cheap mass-production methods, may drive out the traditional arts and crafts. Radio and phonograph threaten to replace the gamelan. Cheap cloth prints might end the hand batik industry, and movies could finish the centuries-old art of the wajang.

There is indeed a danger that the marvelous creative spirit of Indonesian art may suffer from these modern trends. But the friends of Indonesia will hope that—as so many times in the past and in so many different ways—Indonesia may be able in this case also to take from the rest of the world without destroying the fine inner quality of its own artistic life.

12

Language and Education

More than two hundred languages are spoken in Indonesia. They are alike in a number of ways, but each is enough different from the others to be called a separate tongue by scholars. And the three major ones are spoken by enormous numbers: Javanese, forty million; Sundanese, twelve million; Madurese, six million. There are a half dozen more languages spoken by one or two million people each, and many dozen others whose use is confined to a small area.

Yet in spite of this mixture of tongues still used in family and village life in the different sections, the country has managed to gain general acceptance for one national language. That is called Bahasa Indonesia ("the Indonesian language"), and the story of its growth in the last thirty years is truly remarkable.

Usually languages grow slowly and change slowly. Even the daily users often fail to see what is happening to the language they speak. But the growth of the Indonesian language, and its spread over the entire country, resulted from conscious action by the leaders of the freedom movement.

Few cases can be found in history in which a deliberate decision about language has been so successful, and in which the new language has been so quickly adopted by so many people.

All of the languages in Indonesia belong to the general family called Malayo-Polynesian that is found not only in Southeast Asia but also through the Pacific Islands. Even the United States can claim a tiny corner of this vast linguistic empire, because the original language of one of our states, Hawaii, belongs to the same family.

Of the various branches of the language, the one called Malay, though not spoken by the largest number of people, was the accepted way for traders from different areas to talk with each other. Some knowledge of Malay thus spread quite widely, especially in port cities, throughout the Indies. Because of this contact with people from abroad, words from other languages crept into the Malay vocabulary. The resulting dialect was sometimes called "port Malay" or "bazaar Malay," that is, Malay used in the market.

During much of the nearly three centuries of Dutch rule there was precious little education of any kind for Indonesians. Then, under the Ethical Policy at the start of this century, schools were started for Indonesians, but using the Dutch language. The small percentage of people getting an education were almost entirely upper class. They studied Dutch books, wrote in Dutch, and (if they were lucky enough to go abroad for an education at all) went to Dutch universities.

It is ironical, but not surprising, that much of the early protest against foreign rule was not in a local language but in Dutch.

But a great ground swell was coming to the surface among the people themselves. In 1924, for example, a sensation was caused when a cultural hero named Djajadiningrat gave a speech in Malay in the Dutch-sponsored People's Council of which he was a member. Both the largest Muslim party and the Communist Party used Malay, and in 1928 a youth congress declared in favor of one national language. A lively group of young writers started a magazine called *Pudjangga Baru* (New Writer) that helped make the use of Malay fashionable among patriotic intellectuals. Or rather, the language they were promoting was now becoming known as Indonesian.

Because Indonesian is not known in other countries, some world language is needed for access to general knowledge and literature and to conduct foreign business. Before independence Dutch was of course the language used for this purpose. But Dutch is itself a minor language. So in part for that reason and in part because of an emotional turning away from all colonial connections, English was made the official foreign language.

Besides Indonesian and a foreign language, however, Indonesians have their own local languages. To show how far this can go, take the case of a friend of the author who is from the island of Madura. He talks his native Madurese with his mother, Indonesian with business associates, Dutch and Indonesian with his wife who is a Sumatran, Javanese with his children's nursemaid, and excellent English with his American friends. He also has some French and German from school, some Japanese from the time of the occupation, and some Arabic from the Holy Koran.

It seems unfair that people who take to languages so naturally should themselves have one of the easiest. Any readers of this book who have been studying French or Latin or German would be overjoyed with Indonesian. It is a sheer delight for the beginning student, as it is without conjugations, declensions, case-endings, gender-endings, subjunctives, and most of the other usual horrors. There are no articles. Verbs and adjectives do not have the problem of agreement with nouns.

Most of the time there is not even a difference between singular and plural. When the Indonesians have to show a plural idea but no number is mentioned, they repeat the noun. So "buku" means book but "buku-buku" is books. In written or printed form however they usually use a small figure "2" instead of repeating the word: "buku²."

But there is another virtue in the language besides the lovely lack of grammar and the easy pronunciation. There are many words taken from other languages. Some of those are languages we do not know, but there are many others from Latin that are familiar to us through English or French. A large number are Germanic words that reached Indonesia through Dutch, but have similar forms in English. Then there are the words which Indonesia took straight from English, either via British or Yankee traders in the old days or during the Raffles period of British rule, or, in most recent years, from the close contact with America.

We need no dictionary to tell us the meaning of such Indonesian words as universitas, presiden, tilpon, tilgram, Djanuari, Pebruari, industri. And there are words that we might not guess at first but will never forget once we have learned them: *es* for ice; *Inggeris* for English; *priwil* for free-wheel; *pulpen* for fountain pen; *saus* for gravy; *speda motor* for motorcycle; *portret* for photograph; *partikulir* for private. In modern science and technology most of the words come from the same international form, often based on Greek, from which we get our terms in English.

A final comfort of Indonesian for the beginning student is the fact that the language is written in the same roman letters used for English and other European languages. Lest we take that big fact for granted, we should remember that Indonesian is the only major Eastern language except Turkish that is written in our alphabet. Malay was formerly written in the beautiful but difficult Arabic script, reading from right to left.

An interesting thing has happened in relation to Malay, the mother tongue of Indonesian. Malay is the national language of the neighboring country, the Federation of Malaya. Because the Indonesian people outnumber the Malayans about 20 to 1, we might say the daughter has grown much larger than the mother. And the new language is having a strong influence on the old one, just as American English has affected its parent, British English. In the case of the two forms of Malay, however, differences are bigger. Variation in spelling even changed alphabetical order. For instance, the Indonesian sound "tj" was "ch" in Malay. So the two countries signed an agreement in 1960, hoping to iron out those differences.

When the decision for a national language was made, Javanese might have been chosen because it was known to much the largest number of people in the Indies. The nationalists had the vision to see, however, the danger of jealousy on the part of all the non-Java people, the minorities from the other islands, and even the Sundanese and Madurese speakers on Java itself.

But the real objection to Javanese was that it was associated in the public mind with the upper classes. The aristocracy tended in former times to be the only people who were literate in Javanese, and so the language in written form seemed to be for aristocrats. It was less suitable for a modern nation than the down-to-earth Malay. And Javanese is a complex business anyway. There are three different forms of the language, for use when talking to superiors, to inferiors, and to people of your own class. That did not sound like the right way for people to talk in a democracy.

So the new national language based on Malay became more than just a means of communication. It is a symbol of nationhood, and one of the ways in which Indonesia binds together the different parts of its great country. Regional spirit is still strong in Indonesia—in some ways too strong for its own good. But in Indonesia, as in the United States, local pride and loyalty at their best can fit into a larger patriotism. The Kansan or Vermonter who loves his own state is a better American because of that feeling.

Indonesia hopes to achieve the same sort of loyalty that is suggested in the national mottoes of both countries. That implies mutual respect, understanding, and tolerance. It even involves pride in the different culture of fellow citizens in other parts of the country. A Muslim from Sumatra, for instance, takes pride in the Hindu dancing of Bali. A Javanese is delighted by the perfect design of folk art from Celebes or the charm of Minangkabau houses. People from all the islands thrill at the noble Hindu and Buddhist monuments in Java. Muslims in all the islands respect able public servants even though they are Christians from Sumatra. The whole nation honors its heroes from whatever section or religion or way of life.

We talked a great deal about language in this chapter because it is one of the three strongest forces holding the country together. The others, of course, are religion and the love of independence. All three have played a big part in the greatest achievement of the nation since it began. That is education.

In a number of other ways the new country has done poorly. Production has fallen off in several fields, and the economy generally fell into a sad state. The experience with political democracy failed to satisfy Indonesians, let alone critical foreigners. But progress in education, though still needing to be carried much further, has been outstanding.

As we mentioned earlier, the number of people able to read and write has increased from seven per cent of the population to an officially claimed fifty-seven per cent in 1960. The number of elementary schools has jumped two hundred per cent since independence and of secondary schools about nine hundred per cent. At the same time universities, teachers colleges, and technical schools have been started. And, in some ways the most exciting of all, adult "mass education" classes are found through the country.

Nursery schools and kindergartens are seen from time to time. There are only a few hundred thus far, but the number is increasing. They are largely private, sponsored by churches, societies, or individuals. Many of them are run by teachers trained in the U.S. or elsewhere abroad, and they seem much like American schools. They have similar programs of games, singing, arts and crafts, and much of the equipment is very well designed.

In the regular government school system, six years of elementary school are followed by three years of junior high school and three years of senior high school, and then university or professional school. In spite of the great improvements of recent years, the percentage of students reaching the top of the ladder is still very small. Many children still end their schooling with sixth grade or even earlier. High school seems more like a special privilege and a reward of merit than it does with us.

Many of the senior high schools, and even some of those in the junior section, are vocational schools, permitting the start of professional training right after elementary school. Thus, besides the regular schools, there are many that give special training in commercial work, domestic science, mechanics, agriculture, social work, etc.

In the elementary schools especially, but in the high schools also, civics is a major subject. The subject gained special importance because of the effort at spreading grass-roots understanding of government plans.

As might be guessed from comments earlier in this chapter, language has a large place in school studies. In each region the teaching can be in the local language (Javanese, Sundanese, etc.) for the first two years, but the national Indonesian language is studied at the same time. After that, only the national language can be used for teaching; and English and sometimes other foreign languages are subjects of study.

There are fewer student activities than in our schools, but the Indonesians make up for this by the large number of youth groups sponsored by the government or private associations. The Boy Scouts are especially active. In some cities there are organizations like our playground societies for singing, dance, music, and sports.

Indonesians are not content with their schools yet. They are calling all the time for more school buildings, teachers, and books, and for making the quality of education better. Instead of being self-satisfied about the progress made in the first years of the Republic, they think the present school system is only a halfway point toward what they hope for later on. The foreigner, however, sees that to have built a national educational system at all is an accomplishment. It has drawn on efforts through the years by many different groups in Indonesia. And it benefits now from the work of foreign-trained Indonesians as well as foreign specialists sent on Indonesian requests by our government, by American foundations, and by international organizations.

Going along with the great educational trend have been developments in the fields of newspapers, magazines, and book publishing.

Those activities used to be entirely in Dutch hands, and not many Indonesians had previous experience with them. They have taken to the work very naturally, however. There are many problems, of which censorship and paper shortages are the most difficult, but the Indonesians in these fields keep right on with energy and initiative. Some of the Djakarta bookshops are among the best run and most attractive of any in Asia.

Of the foreign books imported in recent years, the largest number have been American, thanks to an arrangement of our government that permits the Indonesians to buy our books with their own money, without having to pay in dollars. English-language books are in any event very popular in Indonesia today, and in many university courses American textbooks are used. Translations of American books into Indonesian are likewise being published.

Although there has been a fair amount of writing in Indonesian, it has lacked the foundation of years of previous literature in the language. Older works were usually in Dutch, and the aristocratic Javanese tradition of writing only for and about the upper classes was not much help. Censorship, economic hardship, and other troubles have brought new problems to writers in recent years. But Indonesian writing seems now to have a base. At least the most important thing for a national literature has been supplied—an audience able to read what is written.

13

Toward the Future

In April, 1955, the West Java city of Bandung became the center of world attention. For a time Bandung swept both Moscow and Washington off the front pages of newspapers, and reporters from every nation on earth were in this delightful Indonesian city that most of them had never heard of a few months before.

Bandung is a charming place, with clean streets and handsome hotels. An American visitor said, "It couldn't have happened to a nicer city." It has been for a long time the center of cultural life of the Sundanese people, and Bandung puppet shows are famous. But these were not the reasons for the world-wide interest.

The occasion was the first meeting ever held of representatives of nearly all the peoples of Asia and Africa. The Bandung Conference was attended by Nehru of India, Nasser of Egypt, and most of the other leaders of the independent or would-be independent countries of the two continents.

Few actions of importance were taken at Bandung, but the conference was nevertheless one of the great dividing points of history.

Before that time the peoples of the two continents, even those who had won full independence, continued to think of themselves as to some extent wards of Europe. At Bandung they suddenly realized their independent power.

But they were also struck, some apparently for the first time, with an awesome sense of their world responsibilities. They seemed in some ways like a student council that has been agitating for years for certain rights and then, having won them, is suddenly faced with the obligations that they had not realized would be handed to them along with the powers. Or one might think of a young American finally getting a driver's license and all at once realizing the responsibility placed on him when at last he finds himself alone behind a wheel.

Many of the world problems that the new countries had happily left to the older nations were now dumped directly on them. Nothing was solved at Bandung, but the meeting marked the coming of age of the movements for national independence in Africa and Asia.

The discussion of imperialism—the rule of colonies by other countries—was especially lively at Bandung. Many of the leaders present were former if not present revolutionists. They were accustomed to striking out at Britain, Holland, and other colonial powers as oppressors of subject peoples. They were so much in the habit that they went right on talking that way at Bandung, even though many of the battles against European imperialists had already been won. Chou En-lai, the adroit delegate of Communist China, naturally did all he could to encourage such talk.

But some of the others, especially the prime minister of Ceylon, pointed out that the end of *that* battle was near, while the imperialism of Mr. Chou and other Communists was an active and rising danger to Asian and African freedom. The conference ended by condemning imperialism of all sorts. This might not seem very sensational, but it was the first time that Asian and African people generally had boldly recognized that the bad old countries of Europe were not the only ones threatening them.

President Sukarno's opening address was, to Americans, of special interest because of the treatment that he gave to our early history. He happened to be speaking on the one hundred eightieth anniversary of the ride of Paul Revere, and American reporters were startled to hear this fact mentioned by the leader of a new nation on the opposite side of the world. Not only did he refer to it, he called our Revolution "the first successful anti-colonial war in history," and he even quoted from Longfellow's poem:

"A cry of defiance and not of fear,
A voice in the darkness, a knock at the door,
And a word that shall echo forevermore!"

"Yes," he continued, "it shall echo forevermore. . . . But remember, that battle which began one hundred eighty years ago is not completely won, and it will not have been completely won until we can survey this our world and say that colonialism is dead."

He mentioned "colonialism in modern dress" as being economic control or intellectual control by powerful groups within a country. Some thought he was talking about Communists; some thought he meant the hold that Dutch and Chinese business and financial interests held over the Indonesian economy, and similar influence in other countries by European and American businessmen.

Since that time the Communists have greatly increased their political following and their influence in Indonesia, many Dutch businesses in the country have been seized by the government, and Chinese businessmen are forbidden to operate outside the cities.

The future is uncertain. Indonesia cut its last ties with Holland, but has received major economic help from both the United States and Communist countries. Economically the country has gone down hill. In the black market, the money unit, the rupiah, brings only a fraction of its official value.

Politically, Indonesia has given up its attempt at representative democracy of the sort we know, and has tried a new plan which is called "guided democracy," with no political parties permitted except those endorsing the system. Because the Communist Party supported the plan, it rose to new prominence, while its former chief opponent, the Masjumi Party, was outlawed. A possible balance wheel is the army, which has been a stable non-Communist influence at several tense moments in the past.

Whatever plan of government Indonesia finally adopts, it is certain that there will be quite a bit of socialism in the economic system. The government will play an active part in many things left to private business in capitalist countries. The social services of a "welfare state" will probably be attempted on a wide scale.

Indonesian socialists felt in the past that they could not accept either straight capitalism, which they believed limited economic freedom, or straight socialism of the Marxist sort, which they knew denied freedom to the individual. They wanted, in time-honored Indonesian style, to see if they could work out a new system of their own, drawing something from both. There has been great interest in Scandinavian "co-operative societies" for that reason. Dr. Hatta and some of his followers made special studies of Sweden's method that they thought might point a middle way for them.

What many Indonesians feared was that the Communists, obedient to foreign control and more interested in world issues than Indonesian welfare, would wipe out all freedom if they should get full control of the government. A reasonable amount of freedom must be preserved if Indonesia is to work out a system adapted to its own conditions.

The country seems to have a new political crisis every month, and the economic crises are so grave and so frequent that, as we have said several times in this book, the world is always wondering how long Indonesia will last.

But Indonesia has survived everything thus far. It can draw on great natural strengths not only of a material sort but of heart and spirit also. The people are highly industrious when there is reason for it. They tend to keep on working at their jobs no matter what is happening in politics. And above all they are patient.

There is an age-old basis of semi-democracy in village life, and there is that spirit of gotong rojong, or mutual help, which we have mentioned before. In spite of the introduction of a "money economy," many of the people outside of the cities live chiefly on what they themselves produce, with few cash purchases the year round. Land ownership is spread widely, and the "landlord problem" is less than in most Asian countries. The tradition of musjawarah, or discussion, can be a happy substitute for trigger-happy action. And the ideal of the revolution's Five Principles (of which belief in God is one of the most basic in this Muslim land) and the tolerant idea of "Unity in Diversity" give the basis for a society that America should be able to understand and endorse.

What we should hope for these attractive and admirable people is no slavish copy of the *details* of our own system. We built ours out of our own history and special conditions. May they do the same, finding a plan which permits an open society with human dignity for its citizens and the fullest life for the individual—in his body, his mind, and his spirit.

INDEX

121